D1482056

STEIN AND DAY PLAY SERIES

THE THE
PRIVATE PUBLIC
EAR EYE

THE
PRIVATE
EAR

TWO PLAYS BY

THE
PUBLIC
EYE

PETER SHAFFER

TEIN AND DAY / *Publishers* / New York

Designed by David Miller.
Printed in the United States of America.

Stein and Day / Publishers / 7 East 48 Street, New York, N. Y. 10017

For
Victor
WITH LOVE

The Private Ear and *The Public Eye* were first presented at the Globe Theatre, London, on May 10, 1962, by H. M. Tennent Ltd., with the following cast:

THE PRIVATE EAR
TED	Douglas Livingstone
BOB	Terry Scully
DOREEN	Maggie Smith

THE PUBLIC EYE
JULIAN	Kenneth Williams
CHARLES	Richard Pearson
BELINDA	Maggie Smith

Lighting by Joe Davis

These plays were first presented in New York at the Morosco Theater on October 9, 1963, by Roger L. Stevens by arrangement with H. M. Tennent, Ltd., with the following cast:

THE PRIVATE EAR
TED	Barry Foster
BOB	Brian Bedford
DOREEN	Geraldine McEwan

THE PUBLIC EYE
JULIAN	Barry Foster
CHARLES	Moray Watson
BELINDA	Geraldine McEwan

Both productions:
Directed by Peter Wood
Decor by Richard Negri

THE
PRIVATE
EAR
A Play in One Act

Characters

BOB

TED

DOREEN

SCENE: BOB's *sitting room in Belsize Park, London. A summer evening, about seven o'clock.*

It is a fairly shabby attic room: the room of a young and rather disorganized bachelor. There is a window at the back looking out over a grimy London roof-scape. Besides the bed, over which hangs a large print of Botticelli's "Birth of Venus," there is a frayed armchair, a chest of drawers, a couple of chairs, and a stool. The room is dominated by the twin speakers of a stereophonic gramophone, attached to the sloping roof on either side of the window.

The machine itself is downstage to the left (audience view) and nearby it are shelves of BOB's *records. Over to the right is the kitchen; through its sliding door can be glimpsed another window opening onto the same flushed sky. The main door to the landing and stairs is downstage, right.*

When the curtain rises music is playing: Mozart on the gramophone. The door bursts open and BOB *dashes in, toweling his head. He is an awkward young man in his late teens, or early twenties, and his whole manner exudes an evident lack of confidence—in himself and in life. Throughout this first scene he displays the greatest agitation and indecision in his preparations. There is an iron plugged into the electric light. He switches it on—then runs to his chest of drawers, unwraps and applies a new deodorant stick. It is evident he has never used one before. He runs to the cupboard for his trousers and then back to the iron to press them—but the iron is still cold. Impatiently the boy sits down to wait.*

Another sort of music is heard approaching. TED *comes in carrying a blaring little transistor and a carrier bag full of shopping.* TED *is about twenty-five, cocky and extroverted, fitted out gaily by Shaftesbury Avenue to match his own inner confidence and self-approval.*

[13]

TED. Christ! D'you know what time it is?

BOB. What?

TED. (*Switching off gramophone and then his own radio*). Seven twenty-two. What the hell have you been up to while I've been doing your shopping? Dreaming, I suppose, as usual.

BOB. I haven't.

TED. You're marvelous! The most important night of your life, and you can't even get yourself dressed. All you can do is listen to bloody music.

BOB. I wasn't listening. It was just on.

TED. I bet. And what are you doing now?

BOB. Pressing my pants. But it won't get hot.

TED. If she's on time you've got eight minutes . . . I bought you some flowers. They'll provide that chic touch you're just a tiny bit in need of up here. (*Getting the vase.*) Did you have a bath?

BOB. Yes.

TED. Did you use that stick I gave you?

BOB. Yes.

TED. I'll do that. You get your shirt on. (*Takes the iron from him and uses it quickly and expertly.*) What are you wearing over that?

BOB. Oh for heaven's sake!

TED. Did you?

BOB. Yes.

TED. I'll do that. You get your shirt on. (*Takes the iron from him and uses it quickly and expertly.*) What are you wearing over that?

BOB. I thought my blazer.

TED. It's a bit schooly, but she'll probably like that. Makes you look boyish. You'll bring out the protective in her. What tie?

BOB. (*Producing a tie*). I thought this.

TED. Oh yes, gorgeous. What is it? The Sheffield Young Men's Prayer Club?

BOB. Don't be daft. What's wrong with it?

TED. You really don't know, do you? Look: that sort of striped tie, that's meant to suggest a club or an old school. Well, it marks you, see? "I'm really a twelve pound a week office worker," it says. "Every day I say, Come on five thirty, and every week I say, Come on Friday night. That's me and I'm contented with my lot." That's what that tie says to me.

BOB. Well you must have very good hearing, that's what I say.

TED. Where's that green shantung one I gave you last Christmas?

BOB. I lost it.

TED. Typical.

BOB. It isn't. I never lose anything.

TED. I think your subconscious would make you lose anything that was chic.

BOB. That's idiotic. And so's that word.

TED. What? Chic?

BOB. Yes. What's it supposed to mean?

TED. It's French for With It.

BOB. With it?

TED. Yes. With It, which is what you're not, and high time you
were. You can't stay in the provinces all your life, you
know. Come on! You've got six minutes . . . You're not
going to let me down tonight, are you?

BOB. What do you mean?

TED. You know what you're going to do this evening? I mean,
you know what I'm expecting you to do, don't you?

BOB. Look, Ted. it's not that way at all.

TED. No?

BOB. No, not at all.

TED. Well then, I'm wasting my time here, aren't I? With all
due respect, mate, there are rival attractions to playing
chef to you, you know. Do you know where I could be
tonight? This very night?

BOB. Where?

TED. With her! (*He produces a photograph.*) Look.

BOB. Goodness!

TED. How about them for a pair of bubbles? And that hair—
you can't keep your hands off it. It's what they call raven.

BOB. Raven?

TED. Raven black. It's got tints of blue in it.

BOB. Where did you meet this one?

TED. In the Whiskey-à-Go-Go, last night, twisting herself giddy with some little nit. I sort of detached her. She wanted a date right away, for tonight, but I said, "Sorry, doll, no can do. I'm engaged for one night only, at great expense, as chef to my mate Tchaik, who is entertaining a bird of his own. Très special occasion." So be grateful. Greater love hath no man than to pass up a bird like this for his mate. Look at the way she holds herself. That's what they used to call "carriage." You don't see too much of that nowadays. Most of the girls I meet think they've got it, ignorant little nits. That is the genuine article, that is. Carriage. (*He sets the photo on the table.*) Miss Carriage.

BOB. What's her name?

TED. You won't believe me if I tell you. Lavinia.

BOB. Lavinia?

TED. Honest. How's that for a sniff of class? The rest of it isn't so good. Beamish. Lavinia Beamish.

BOB. She's beautiful.

TED. Do you think so?

BOB. Yes.

TED. She's going to go off fairly quickish. In three years she'll be all lumpy, like old porridge.

BOB. I don't know how you do it. I don't, honest.

TED. Just don't promise them anything, that's all. Make no promises, they can't hang anything on you, can they?

BOB. I wouldn't know.

[17]

TED. Well, you're going to, after tonight.

BOB (*Exasperated*). Ted! Please . . .

TED. Here, I heard a good one the other day. The National Gallery just paid ten thousand pounds for a picture of a woman with five breasts. D'you know what it's called?

BOB. What?

TED. "Sanctity."

BOB (*Not understanding*). Sanctity.

TED. Un, deux, trois, quatre, cinq . . . What do you call this, laying a table?

BOB. What's wrong with it?

TED. So we're all left-handed?

BOB. Oh lord. (*He hurries to re-lay the table. In his haste he upsets the vase. He stares at the mess.*)

TED. You've got the pit-a-pats, haven't you? Well, get a cloth.

(BOB *scurries to get it.*)

You've wet my Lavinia. We'll have to dry you out, love. (*He crosses and puts the photograph in the corner of Bob's mirror.*)

Now look, Tchaik: if you get in a state, the evening will be a fiasco. So sit there and calm down.

BOB (*Biting his nails*). I am calm.

TED (*Producing nail clippers*). Don't ruin your appetite. After all, this is just a girl, isn't it? Even if you say she looks like a Greek goddess, she's still only flesh and blood.

BOB. What time do you make it?

TED. Seven thirty, just gone.

BOB. Do you think she's not coming?

TED. Of course she's coming. It's a free dinner, isn't it? I hope you've put clean sheets on this bed.

BOB. Oh, Ted, I wish you'd stop talking like that.

TED. Look: let's get things a bit clear. You go to hundreds of concerts. This is the first time you've picked up a bird and invited her home for fried chicken and vino, isn't it?

BOB. I didn't pick her up. She was sitting next to me and dropped her program.

TED. On purpose.

BOB. Don't be silly. She's not that sort.

TED. Everyone's that sort.

BOB. Well she isn't. I just know.

TED. Well what's wrong if she did? She wanted to get to know you. It's just possible, you know, that someone might want to get to know you.

BOB (*Uncomfortably*). Don't be daft.

TED (*Softer*). You might try believing that, Tchaik.

(*A tiny pause. Ted sits too.*)

BOB. In any case, I didn't pick her up. That's a ridiculous expression, anyway. Sort of suggests weightlifting.

TED. What did you do, then?

BOB. Well, I asked her if she liked music. It was a daft question really, because she wouldn't have been at a concert otherwise, would she? It turned out that she was on her own; so I asked her to have a coffee with me after. I could hardly believe it when she said yes.

TED. Why not? Even goddesses get thirsty.

BOB. We went to an expresso bar in Kensington.

TED. And held hands over the brown sugar.

BOB. Not exactly. As a matter of fact, I couldn't think of anything to say to her. We just sat there for a little while and then left.

TED. So that's why you asked me here tonight? To help out with the talk?

BOB. Well you know what to say to women. You've had the practice.

TED. There's no practice needed. Just keep it going, that's all. Bright and not too dirty. The main thing is to edge it subtly towards where you want it to go. You know. In your case you'll be able to start off with music—"What a nice concert that was. I do like Mozart so much, don't you?" Then if she's got any sense at all she'll say, "Oh yes, he does things to me!" and you'll say, "What kind of things?"— and you're off to the races. I'll give you a tip that usually works a treat. After a couple of hours, if she asks for a cigarette, don't give it to her; light it in your mouth and then hand it to her. It's very intimate.

BOB. I don't smoke.

TED. Well you'll have to work out your own style, of course.

BOB. What's it matter? She's not coming anyway.

TED (*Sarcastic*). Of course not.

BOB. I mean it. Look at the time. It's nearly quarter to eight. (*He stands up nervously.*) She's thought better of it, I bet you.

TED. Oh, don't be silly. Most girls think it's chic to be a little late. They think it makes them more desirable. It's only a trick.

BOB. No, that's not her. She doesn't play tricks. That's why all that stuff is so silly—all this plotting: I say this, and she says that. I think things should just happen between people.

TED. Oh, yes. And how many times have they just happened with you?

BOB. Well, that depends on what you want to happen.

TED. You know bloody well what you want to happen.

BOB (*Urgently*). I don't. I don't. This isn't the sort of girl you can make plots about. It would be all wrong. Because she's sort of inaccessible. Pure—but not cold. Very warm.

TED. And you know all this after ten minutes silence in a coffee bar?

BOB. You can know things like that without talking. She's not a talker—she's a listener. That can be more profound, you know. And she's got a look about her—not how people are, but how they ought to be. Do you know when I said about a goddess, do you know who I was thinking of? Her.

TED. Venus?

BOB. She's got exactly the same neck—long and gentle. That's a sign.

TED. What the hell for?

BOB. Spiritual beauty. Like Venus. That's what that picture really represents. The birth of beauty in the human soul. My Botticelli book says so. Listen.

(*He picks up a Fontana pocket book and reads.*)

"Venus, that is to say Humanity, is a nymph of excellent comeliness, born of heaven. Her soul and mind are Love and Charity. Her eyes, Dignity. Her hands, Liberality. Her feet, Modesty." All signs, you see. "Venus is the Mother of Grace, of Beauty, and of Faith."

TED. And this bird of yours is the mother of all that?

BOB. No, of course not. Stop trying to make me into a fool. What I mean is, that look of hers is ideal beauty, Ted. It means she's got grace inside her. Really beautiful people are beautiful inside them. Do you see?

TED. You mean like after taking Andrews Liver Salts?

BOB. Yes, that's exactly what I mean.

TED. Oh, Tchaik, now seriously, come off it. That's all a lot of balls, and you know it. There's a lot of dim, greedy little nitty girls about who are as pretty as pictures.

BOB. I don't mean pretty. I mean . . . well, what you called carriage, for instance. What your Lavinia's got. It's not just something you learn, the way to walk and that. It's something inside you. I mean real carriage, the way you see some girls walk, sort of pulling the air around them like clothes—you can't practice that. You've got first to love the world. Then it comes out.

(*Tiny pause.*)

TED. You poor nut.

BOB. What d'you mean?

TED. Nut. Nut.

BOB. Why?

TED. Oh, dear for you.

(*The door bell rings.*)

BOB. God! There she is.

(*He dashes about on a last second tidy of the flat.* TED *watches, amused.* BOB *grabs his blazer.*)

TED. Now listen. Last swallow of coffee and I'm away. Leave you to it. 9:30 you'll see me. 9:31 you won't. Work to do at home? Get it? Now—where is the bottle of Dubonnet?

(BOB *says nothing.*)

It's the one thing I left you to do.

BOB. I know. I forgot.

TED. You nit! Now you've nothing to give her for a cocktail.

(*The bell rings again.*)

BOB. What am I going to do?

TED. Well, there's nothing you can do, is there? Just don't mention it, that's all. Say nothing about it. She comes from the suburbs. She probably won't expect anything. Wine at dinner will impress her enough.

BOB. Oh hell.

TED. Why don't you leave her standing there? She'll go away in five minutes.

(BOB *dashes out.* TED *gives the room a final look-over, elaborately combs his hair in the mirror, and then strolls into the kitchen. Steps are heard running upstairs.* TED *quickly shuts the kitchen door as* BOB *returns with* DOREEN, *a pretty girl of about twenty, wearing an imitation ocelot coat. It is at once obvious that she is as nervous as he is and has no real pleasure in being there. Her reactions are anxious and tight, and these, of course, do nothing to reassure* BOB.)

DOREEN. I'm not late?

BOB. No. Just right. It's just half past seven. You're very punctual.

DOREEN. Unpunctuality's the thief of time, as my dad says.

BOB. To coin a phrase.

DOREEN. Pardon?

BOB. Can I take your coat?

DOREEN. Thank you.

   (*She slips it off. Under it she is wearing a jumper and skirt.*)

BOB (*Taking the coat*). That's pretty.

DOREEN. D'you like it?

BOB. I do, yes. Is it real? I mean real leopard.

DOREEN. It's ocelot.

BOB. (*Hanging it up*). Oh! (*Imitating* TED.) Very chic.

DOREEN. Pardon?

BOB. Won't you sit down?

(*They advance into the room.*)

DOREEN. Thanks. Is this all yours? Or do you share?

BOB. No, I live alone.

DOREEN (*Looking at the table*). But you've got three places.

BOB. Actually, there's a friend here at the moment. He's helping with the dinner. We work in the same office.

DOREEN. Can I do anything?

BOB. No. it's all done. Really. All you can do is sit down and relax. (*With an attempt at "style" he gestures at the arm-chair.*)

DOREEN. Thanks. (DOREEN *sits in it. A tiny pause.*)

BOB. Do you smoke?

DOREEN. I do a bit, yes.

BOB. Good! Tipped or plain? (*He picks up a cigarette box and opens it with a flourish.*)

DOREEN. Well! There's luxury for you, isn't it—both kinds! Tipped, thank you.

BOB. Allow me.

(*He picks up a lighter with his other hand and tries to snap it alight. It doesn't work. He puts down the box and fumbles with it, to no avail.*)

DOREEN. It's all right, I've got a match.

(*He sits. Another tiny pause.*)

BOB. So, how have you been?

DOREEN. Fine. You?

BOB. Yes. Can't complain. Er . . . you're a typist, aren't you?

DOREEN. Stenographer. The place that trained me said, "Never call yourself a typist: it's degrading."

BOB. Oh. What kind of things do you—well, stenog, I suppose?

DOREEN. The usual letters.

BOB. Yours of the tenth?

DOREEN. Pardon?

BOB. "Dear sir, in reply to yours of the tenth." Things like that?

DOREEN. Oh, I see. Yes, that's right.

BOB. Do you mind it?

DOREEN. What?

BOB. Doing the same thing, day in, day out.

DOREEN. Well there's not much choice, is there?

BOB. I suppose not.

DOREEN. You've got to earn your living, haven't you? Like my dad says, "Money doesn't grow on trees."

BOB. No . . . Wouldn't they look funny if it did?

DOREEN. Pardon?

BOB. The trees. The trees.

DOREEN. Oh, yes. (*She looks at him nervously.*)

BOB (*Plunging on*). Like when people say unpunctuality's the thief of time—like your dad says. I always used to imagine unpunctuality in a mask—you know—with a sack labeled "swag." That's what comes of having a literal mind. I remember I had awful trouble at school one day with that poem which says, "The child is father of the man." I simply couldn't see it. I mean how could a child be a father? I couldn't get beyond that. I don't think imagination's a thing you can cultivate though, do you? I mean, you're either born with it or you're not.

DOREEN. Oh yes, you're born with it.

BOB. Or you're not.

DOREEN. No.

BOB. Mind you, I think there ought to be a sign so parents can tell. There probably is, if we knew how to read it. I mean, all babies are born with blue eyes, aren't they?

DOREEN. Yes.

BOB. But no one ever says there's a difference in the blue. And I bet there is. I bet if you looked really hard at six babies the first day they were born you'd see six different kinds of blue. Milky blue—sharp blue, you know, like corn-flower color—petrol blue—peacock blue . . . And they each mean something different about character. Course, that's the first day, and then they all fade and become the same. (*Pause. He looks at her unhappily.*) It's a thought, anyway.

DOREEN. Oh yes!

BOB. A daft one. Would you like a drink?

DOREEN. Well, I wouldn't say no.

BOB (*Realizing too late that he has no drink*). Good! . . . What would you like?

DOREEN. Whatever you suggest. I'm not fussy.

BOB. Dubonnet?

DOREEN. That'd be lovely.

BOB. Well, if you'll just excuse me. (*He starts emptying an old whiskey bottle, containing a collection of shillings, on the dresser.*)

DOREEN. What are you doing?

BOB. I won't be a minute.

DOREEN. Can I help?

BOB. I won't be a second.

DOREEN. Where are you going?

BOB. Just downstairs. To the pub. It's only a step away.

DOREEN. Haven't you got any in?

BOB. No—I don't drink.

DOREEN. You don't?

BOB. No.

DOREEN. Well, don't go on my account.

BOB. That's all right. I mean, I want to.

DOREEN. That's silly.

BOB. Why?

DOREEN. Because I don't drink either.

BOB. You're only just saying that.

DOREEN. No, honest, I don't.

BOB. Ever?

DOREEN. Well, only on special occasions, at Christmas and that. But I don't want one now. I only said it to be sociable.

BOB. You're sure?

DOREEN. Positive.

BOB. Well, that's all right then.

(*Enter* TED *with two glasses of wine on tray, playing the waiter.*)

TED. Cocktails, madame?

DOREEN (*Delighted*). Ohh!

BOB. Ted, this is my friend, the one I told you about. Miss Marchant.—Ted Veasey.

TED. Pleased to meet you.

DOREEN. How d'you do?

TED. All the better for seeing you, thank you. You know, most people never answer that question—how do you do? That's because those who ask it don't really want to know. How do *you* do?

DOREEN (*Beginning to giggle*). Oh: very nicely, thank you.

TED. That's all right then. Do I have to call you Miss?

DOREEN. Well, it is a bit formal, isn't it? Why don't you call me Doreen?

TED. Thanks, I will. If it's not too presumptuous. You see, I'm only the butler around here.

(*Offers her a drink.*)

Doreen? A little chilled vino avant le diner?

DOREEN (*Hesitating to take one*). Well . . .

BOB. I'm afraid she doesn't drink.

TED. No?

DOREEN. Well, only on special occasions.

TED. Well tonight's an occasion, isn't it? Of course, it is. A real proper (*French*) "occasion"! Come on. Do you good.

DOREEN. Well . . . Just to be sociable.

TED. That's it.

(*Offering drink to* BOB.)

Tchaik?

BOB. Not for me. You know I don't.

TED. Come on, it's a special occasion.

DOREEN. Come on, I'm having one.

BOB. I don't think I will, not on an empty stomach.

TED (*Drinks*). Well, waste not, want not, I say! The servants you get these days! Well, the chicken awaits. I'd better go and wring its neck. (*Exit.*)

DOREEN. He's funny.

BOB. Yes, he is. He's marvelous to have in the office. Always cheerful.

DOREEN. Aren't you?

BOB. Not always, no.

DOREEN. What office do you work for?

BOB. Import-export. I'm just a glorified office boy really. At least that's what Ted keeps on telling me, and I suppose he's right.

DOREEN. Why, is he above you?

BOB. In a way he is, yes.

DOREEN. What way?

BOB. Well, he's just been promoted to look after a small department of his own. It means quite a bit of responsibility. He's going to go a long way, I think. I mean he's interested and keen—you know.

DOREEN. Aren't you?

BOB. Well, not so much as he is. He knows all about economics. Tariffs and all that. I'm afraid it's all rather beyond me.

DOREEN. I like people who want to get on. Who've got drive. That's something I respect. My dad's got drive.

BOB. What does he do?

DOREEN. Well, he's retired now. He used to be a foreman in a factory.

BOB. Where?

DOREEN. Edmonton.

BOB. Oh.

DOREEN. He says, if you haven't got drive, you might as well be dead.

BOB. He's probably right. Is that drink all right?

DOREEN. Yes, it's lovely.

BOB. Good.

DOREEN. Cheerio.

BOB. Cheerio.

DOREEN. This is a nice room.

BOB. D'you like it?

DOREEN. It must be nice, living high up.

BOB. It is. And they're very tolerant here.

DOREEN. Tolerant?

BOB. I mean, they don't interfere with your private weaknesses—you know.

DOREEN. Pardon?

BOB. I mean your habits. I'm afraid I've got rather a weakness and some people would get a bit irritable about it, but not here. They let me play Behemoth all night long. (*Indicating the stereophonic machine.*) This is him, of course. Behemoth means a great monster, you know. It's in the Bible.

DOREEN. What is it then, a gramophone?

BOB. Stereo.

DOREEN. It looks lovely.

BOB (*A new note of warmth and pride in his voice*). You should hear him. Do you know anything about these animals?

DOREEN. I'm afraid not, no.

BOB. Well, I won't bother you with technical names then. But I can tell you this is really the best machine a chap of my means could possibly afford, anywhere in the world. Of course, if you want to spend thousands it'd be different.

(*With an uncontrollable burst of true enthusiasm, the boy is off on his hobbyhorse.*)

Behemoth's a real marvel, I can tell you. Most big machines you can't play properly below a certain volume. You can't hear them properly unless they blast you out of your seat. That's because they've got bad speakers. (*Indicating.*) These things. Most speakers have only got between five and seven per cent efficiency. These have got between fifteen to twenty. Wharfedale Speakers. They're the best! . . . I'm sorry: I promised not to give you technical names. It's the music that counts anyway, isn't it? (*With great warmth.*) I'm glad you like music. I can't tell you how glad I am to know that. You know, last week I'd been watching you for ages before you dropped that program. I was watching you all through the Bach: and you were so wrapped up in listening, so concentrating, there were wrinkles all over your face!

(*She looks at him, startled and displeased. He falters.*)

well, I mean, they were very becoming . . . I love to see lines on people's faces. I mean, that's their life, isn't it? It's what's happened to them. Most girls you see have got so much powder and muck on, you can't tell anything's happened to them. You know, they're like eggs, their skins. Eggshells, I mean . . . You're different.

DOREEN. You mean I've got inner beauty.

BOB. Do I?

DOREEN. I knew a fellow once who said I had inner beauty. It was his way of saying he was sick of me.

BOB. That's not what I meant at all . . . (*Plunging on.*) You must have been listening to music for an awfully long time to like Bach. Most people come to him only after a bit. When I first started it was all the *Symphonie Pathetique* and *Swan Lake*. You know.

DOREEN (*Who has heard of this*). Oh—yes!

BOB. That's why Ted calls me "Tchaik": It's short for Tchaikovsky. I was mad about his music once. I thought Bach was boring, like exercises. Then one day I was shaving—isn't it daft how things come to you?—I always play records when I'm shaving or in the bath—and I'd put on one of the Brandenburgs, you know, the Fourth with two flutes, and suddenly—just suddenly I heard what made it marvelous. It wasn't about love or victory, or those romantic things that change all the time. It was about things that don't change. D'you see what I mean?

(*She gives him a quick, tight smile, but says nothing.*)

Anyway would you like to hear one? I've got all six.

DOREEN. Lovely . . .

BOB. Good. Well, if you wouldn't mind moving to over here, you'd enjoy it better. You'd be midway between the two speakers at just the right distance. Which Brandenburg would you like?

DOREEN. Well, to be frank, I don't know that much about it. All that old stuff isn't really me.

BOB. You mean you prefer Modern?

DOREEN (*Seeing a gleam of hope*). That's right.

BOB. What d'you like? Stravinsky? Shostakovich?

DOREEN. Well, I don't quite mean that.

BOB. You mean something more tuneful?

DOREEN. Yes.

BOB. Benjamin Britten! Like me. I think Britten's the greatest composer in the world. I mean, he writes tunes, not just plink-plonk. I hate all that twelve-tone stuff, don't you? It's sort of not—human. I know what I'll play you! (*Grabbing an album.*) *Peter Grimes!* Decca's done the most marvelous recording of it. D'you know it?

DOREEN. I can't say I do.

BOB. Oh you'll love it! It's the most wonderful thing you ever heard! It's all about this lonely fisherman who lives by himself, and the village hates him because he's different and has dreams and visions about what life should be. He dreams about this girl, Ellen—someone to share his life, you know, only he's not very good at expressing himself. In the end the village turns against him and accuses him of killing his apprentice. There's a sort of manhunt at night, people calling and shouting, hurrying in with lanterns, making up a posse—you know: it's terrifying. It's like a rising sea, getting wilder and wilder, up and up and up till it suddenly bursts over the town!

(*Taking the record carefully out of its sleeve and putting it on the turntable.*)

I think it's the most marvelous thing I ever heard. Listen!

(*He puts on the record at the moment in Act 3 of* Peter Grimes *when the lynch chorus is finishing its dangerous song of hate—"Him who despises us we'll destroy!"*

BOB *listens to it, entranced, beating time to its hurtling rhythm and mouthing the words, which he clearly knows.*

DOREEN *watches him with something much less like involvement: she obviously detests the music.* BOB *has put it on very loudly: it becomes quite deafening as it boils up into the great shouts of "Peter Grimes!" punctuated by silence.*)

(*Explaining in a hushed voice*). That's his name, "Peter Grimes." They all just stand there and call it. Sssh . . .

(*The chorus yells "Grimes!"* TED *comes in from the kitchen carrying a tray of soup: on his head is a chef's hat made from a grocery bag.*)

TED (*Facetiously*). Did someone call me?

(DOREEN *laughs. He goes over to the table and distributes the soup. Another crash from "Grimes."*)

Turn it down for God's sake, or you'll have the neighbors in. Come on, dinner up! Madame!

DOREEN (*Rising*). Lovely. Thanks very much.

(BOB, *his face set, stops the gramophone.* DOREEN *laughs delightedly and sits herself at the table.*

TED *shakes out a napkin and spreads it over her lap.*

BOB *is very elaborately switching off the set and putting the records back in its sleeve. His movements are slow and mechanical.*)

TED. Hey, Tchaik, stop fussing with that damn thing, and come and be host. It's your party, isn't it? Potage à la Heinz! Champignon! Note that g-n sound, that's pronouncing it proper. Followed by chicken à la Ted Veasey.

(BOB *approaches the table, and with a sudden spurt of aggressiveness, suddenly holds out his glass.*)

TED. Well! What d'you know! He's going to have some after all!

DOREEN. Good for you!

TED (*Pouring him wine*). Here you are, then. The first drop on the long road to ruin!

DOREEN. Cheers!

BOB. Cheers!

TED. That's better! You know, how you stand that stuff I'll never know. Opera! How so-called intelligent people can listen to it I just can't imagine. I mean, who ever heard of people singing what they've got to say?

(*Singing to the Toreador Song in* Carmen.)

"Will you kindly pass the bread?" "Have a bowl of soup?" "Champignon"—"I must go and turn off the gas." Well for heaven's sake! If that's not a bloody silly way to go on, excuse language, I don't know what is. I wish someone would explain it to me, honest. I mean, I'm probably just dead ignorant.

BOB (*Speaking very quietly*). You are.

(TED *looks at him in surprise.* BOB *has never said anything like this before.*)

Dead ignorant.

(*A brief pause.* DOREEN *looks anxiously from one to the other.*)

TED (*Smiling*). Come on. Drink up before it gets cold.

(*All three lift their spoons. They freeze. The lights go down.* BOB *alone is visible sitting in a spot. The next pieces of dialogue are ON TAPE*).

ON TAPE

DOREEN. Ooh, lovely soup! Is it mushroom?

TED. Of course not, it's toadstool.

DOREEN (*Giggling*). Ooh.

TED. My own creation, Mademoiselle, especially for you. It's an old French recipe—only I left out the garlic.

DOREEN. Why?

TED. Well, you never know how the evening might end.

DOREEN. Oh, you are saucy!

(*The dialogue becomes a high-pitched gabble as the tape is deliberately speeded up.* BOB *puts down his spoon and drinks off an entire glass of wine, quickly. He picks up his spoon again, and freezes.*)

Ooh, lovely! Chicken!

TED. Do you like it?

DOREEN. It's my favorite, actually, is chicken. But I could never make up my mind what I wanted—the breast or the leg.

TED. Yes, I know what you mean.

(*Again the conversation moves into a high-pitched gabble.* BOB *empties the bottle of wine into his glass and drinks it, then freezes again.*)

DOREEN. Ooh lovely! . . . What is it?

TED. Passion fruit.

DOREEN. What?

TED. That's its name—passion fruit.

DOREEN (*Coyly*). I don't think I ought to have any.

TED. Go on. One mouthful and you become a hopeless slave of desire.

DOREEN. I think you're pulling my leg.

TED. I wouldn't mind trying.

DOREEN. Pardon?

TED. What time is it then? What time is it then? What time is it then? . . .

(*Echo.*)

What time is it then?

END OF TAPE.

BOB. Nine o'clock.

(*They lower their spoons and resume the scene as the lights come up. Bob sits perfectly still, half in a world of his own.*)

TED. Some more vino, then?

DOREEN. I don't mind if I do.

TED (*Picking up the bottle*). Well, what d'you know? There isn't any. Tchaik's taken it all!

DOREEN. He hasn't. I thought he didn't drink.

TED. Not on an empty stomach. You certainly make up for it on a full one. You want to watch it, mate. Alcohol isn't really a stimulant at all, you know. It's a depressant. It depresses you. That's something most people don't know.

DOREEN. My dad says, "Drink is the curse of the working classes."

TED. Does he?

DOREEN. Yes. Mind you, he can't drink himself because of his ulcer. He suffers from it terribly. Well, of course, he's a natural worrier. Worries about everything.

TED. Does he worry about you?

DOREEN (*Primly*). He's got nothing to worry about in that department, thank you.

TED. No?

DOREEN. No. I mean politics. Things like that. The way the world's going. I think his ulcer started the day he was appointed Branch Secretary of the Union.

TED. Well, that's enough to worry anybody. He's a Union man, then?

DOREEN (*Proudly*). All his life.

TED. Well good luck to him.

DOREEN (*Indignant*). What do you mean?

TED. I'm a Young Conservative myself.

DOREEN (*Suddenly hostile*). I thought so.

TED. I don't care who knows it. Bloody unions. If you ask
me, they're doing their best to ruin the country. Wherever
you look you come back to the same thing, the Unions.
Always at the bottom of everything, the Unions, demanding, demanding, demanding all the time. They make
me bloody sick.

DOREEN. Well I don't agree with you there.

TED. No?

DOREEN. No I don't. My dad can remember the time when
he had to fight to get twopence halfpenny a week.

TED. Your dad?

DOREEN. Yes, my dad!

TED. And how old a gentleman would he be, may one ask?

DOREEN. Well, he's getting on now.

TED. How old?

DOREEN (*Defeated*). Sixty-one.

TED. Well, there you are, then. That's all in the past. It's all
so old-fashioned, the bosses against the workers. I can
tell you one thing, if the Unions are going to run this
country I'm moving out. Because the rate they're going,
they're going to bankrupt it completely and utterly
inside ten years.

BOB (*Dreamily*). There's a notice in the pub next door that
says, "Work is the curse of the drinking classes."

(*A pause.*)

DOREEN. Pardon?

BOB. It's a joke.

TED (*To* DOREEN). Come on, luv, give us a hand.

(*Singing again to* CARMEN.)

"That really was a very lovely meal. I'll collect the mats . . ."

DOREEN (*Singing*). "The knives and forks and spoons."

(TED *takes tray to the kitchen, whistling.*)

TED. Well, at least make the coffee, Tchaik—I'm worn out.

(BOB *rises, unsteadily. He moves to the kitchen.*)

You'd better put your head under the tap.

(BOB *goes into kitchen and* TED *shuts the door on him.*)

How d'you like old Tchaik?

DOREEN. He's nice.

TED. Certainly is. And a very good son to his old mother, let me tell you.

DOREEN. Which is more than you are, I bet.

TED. Me? I look after Number One.

DOREEN. I'm sure.

TED. Well, the way I look at it, I'm enough to look after. I haven't got time to take on anyone else. Anyway, Tchaik's lucky; his old lady lives in Sheffield. Anyone can be a good son to someone living in Sheffield. He goes up there, has a couple of days, high tea, tripe and onions, quick kiss, and he's away. Now me, my people live practically on the doorstep. Wimbledon. Well, that's different, isn't it? "Why can't you live at home?" they say. Home! . . . You're a very lucky girl, you know.

DOREEN. Me?

TED. To have a sensible old dad like yours. You should meet mine—Mr. Alcohol, 1934. That's when he decided draught beer was the secret of life. Well, not decided exactly. He hasn't decided anything since he married Mum. And he was pushed into that by me. She's not much better, mind.

DOREEN. Your mum?

TED. I was a middle-aged slave, or Seven Years in a Bingo Hall. That's when she bothers to go out at all. Mostly she stays in with Twenty Questions and a half bottle of gin. Am I shocking you?

DOREEN. No, not at all. I think it's all very sad.

TED. Do you?

DOREEN. Yes.

TED. I bet there's a lot of fun in you once you loosen up.

DOREEN. Pardon?

TED. What do you think of me?

DOREEN. Well, if you're like most boys, your mind's on just one thing.

TED. Well, I'm not like most boys, I'm me. And my mind's on a lot of things. What's your mind on most of the time? That's when you're not looking after your old dad or going to concerts. What's with that, anyway—I don't get it. You're not the concerty type.

DOREEN. You know it all, don't you?

TED. Well, are you?

DOREEN. No, as a matter of fact, I was given the ticket by a girl friend. She couldn't go and it seemed silly to waste it. (*Indicating the kitchen.*) Now he thinks I'm a music lover, and know about Bach and everythng. Actually it was ever so boring.

(TED *laughs loudly.*)

I realized I shouldn't have said "Yes" to him for tonight as soon as he asked me.

TED. What made you?

DOREEN. Well, I don't know. I don't get out that much. And he was ever so nice and courteous.

TED. I bet.

DOREEN. A blooming sight more better mannered than what you are!

TED. Well who's denying it? Tchaik's always had manners. He's one of Nature's gentlemen.

DOREEN. You're wicked, you know.

TED. I mean it. He's a good boy. He wouldn't hurt a fly— and that's not because he's a fly himself either. Because he isn't. He's got feelings inside him I wouldn't know anything about—and you neither.

DOREEN. Thanks.

TED. I mean it. Real deep feelings. They're no use to him, of course. They're in his way. If you ask me, you're better off without all that dreamy bit.

DOREEN. What d'you mean?

TED. Dreams. Ideas about perfect women. He's got one about you.

DOREEN. He hasn't.

TED. Why d'you think you're here? How many girls do you think he's invited here before?

DOREEN. I dunno.

TED. None (*Spelling it.*) N-O-N-E.

DOREEN. Well, what's he want with me then?

TED. Nothing. You're a vision. You've got a long neck like Venus coming out of the sea.

DOREEN. Who's she?

TED (*Shows picture*). He thinks that you are the living image of her.

DOREEN. Oh—she hasn't got any clothes on—Anyway, I haven't got a long neck like that.

TED. I know you haven't. Yours is the standard size, but he won't leave it at that. He's got to stretch it a bit. A long neck's a sign of a generous nature.

DOREEN. He's a bit nutty, isn't he?

TED. Not really. It's just the old Celtic Twilight in his blood.

DOREEN. Twilight?

TED. Just a phrase.

DOREEN. You don't half have a way of putting things. You've got a gift for words, haven't you?

TED. Always had. Words, languages. It's why I took up French in the evenings.

DOREEN (*Admiringly*). I like that.

TED. Do you? Most people would say I was getting above myself. Then most people just don't count. They've got no drive, no ambition, nothing. I could never be serious about a girl who was one of that lot, could I?

DOREEN. I don't think you could be serious about anyone.

TED. That's where you are wrong, then. That's where you are completely and utterly wrong. You don't know me. I could be serious about someone if she helped me to go places . . . She'd have to have a bit of fun in her too, mind. You ever been to the Whiskey-à-Go-Go?

(BOB *opens the kitchen door, hears the ensuing sentences, and stands listening, the tray of coffee in his hands.*)

DOREEN. No.

TED. You'd like that. I'll take you there if you like.

DOREEN. When?

TED. Any time. You name it.

DOREEN. Well, I'm not sure I'd like it.

TED. 'Course you would. It's all good clean fun. No caveman stuff. None of that touch-you-up and look the other way, honest. I'll take you there next Friday.

DOREEN. No, next Friday I'm busy.

TED. Friday after that, then? Well?

DOREEN (*Suddenly capitulating*). All right.

TED. Good. You'd better give me your phone number, then.

DOREEN. No, I'll meet you there.

TED. I can't have you going there on your own. I'll have to pick you up. That's if you don't live in Norwood, or some lousy place like that.

DOREEN. No. Putney.

TED. You're lucky. That's just inside my cruising area. (*Serious.*) You're all right, you know. You've got it.

DOREEN. Got what?

TED. Oh, that certain something. It used to be called "carriage." People nowadays call it class, but it's not quite the same thing.

(*Suddenly* BOB *comes boldly in with the tray of coffee cups and a pot and sets it down on the sideboard.*)
(*Seeing him: with false breeziness*). Well—I'm away! I'll just have my coffee, and allez. Love you and leave you.

DOREEN. (*Disappointed*). Oh! Why?

TED (*Executive voice*). Duty calls. All that work I took home from the office, clamoring for my attention!

DOREEN. Go on!

TED. Well, that's my story, and I'm stuck with it. No sugar?

BOB. Sorry. (*He goes back into the kitchen.*)

[47]

TED. Cigarette?

DOREEN. No, thank you.

TED (*Offering her the pack*). Go on.

DOREEN. No, really.

TED (*Sotto voce*). Telephone.

DOREEN. What?

TED (*Through clenched teeth*). Number.

DOREEN (*Understanding*). Oh. You got a pencil?—

(BOB *returns.* TED *walks away casually.* DOREEN *is very flustered.*)

It's lovely coffee. It tastes really continental. Like it was bubbling away for hours in one of those machines. Italian . . .

(*An embarrassed pause.* DOREEN *looks helplessly across at* TED *and becomes aware that he has slipped a pencil into her bag.*)

Can I have the little girl's room?

BOB. It's out on the landing. I'll show you.

DOREEN (*Grabbing her handbag*). It's all right. I can find it.

(DOREEN *runs out of the room.* BOB *closes the door. The boys look at one another in silence.*)

TED (*Nervously*). What are you playing at? I've been knocking myself out keeping things going here. What the hell were you doing in the kitchen all that time?

BOB (*Bluntly*). Listening to you.

TED. Well . . . you heard me giving her the chat, then. You know how she feels about you. She thinks you're the most courteous man she's ever met. And so you are, mate. Just don't overdo it, that's all. This is a girl, not a goddess. Just you give her a shove off her pedestal. You'll find she won't exactly resent it.

BOB. Any more advice?

TED. Are you all right?

BOB. That's like "How do you do," isn't it? No answer expected.

TED. Now look, don't start those pit-a-pats going again. This is the critical moment. If you louse this up, I'm going to be very upset.

BOB. Are you?

TED. Well of course. I've gone to no little trouble to set this up for you. Flowers—vino—cooking the dinner—the old sexy dance afterwards to get her in the proper receptive mood. And all for you.

BOB. For me.

TED. Of course. That's why you asked me here, isn't it? To give you the benefit of my savoir-faire.

BOB (*Suddenly exploding*). Savoir-faire! D'you know something? You're so ignorant it's pathetic.

TED. Ignorant? That's twice in one night. If I'm so ignorant I'd better take myself off.

BOB. (*Opening the door*). Why don't you?

TED. Ignorant! That's lovely, that is. Well, I'll know better next time, won't I? I'll know better than to ever help anyone again.

BOB. You don't know what help is. You do your best as you see it, but what if that's nothing, what you see? You'll have lived in vain.

(TED *slams the door violently.*)

TED. Don't you lecture me, boy. It's not me who doesn't help. It's you, who doesn't want it. Maybe that's your whole bit, Tchaik. You *want* it all to be a bloody total disaster. Christ knows why. Well, you've got your wish.

BOB (*Turning on him*). That's all very clever, Ted, but it doesn't mean anything at all. D'you think I'm half-witted?

TED. Of course not.

BOB (*Violently*). Yes you do! That's it! I'm just someone to look down on, aren't I? Teach tricks to. Like a bloody monkey. You're the organ grinder, and I'm the monkey! And that's the way you want people. Well—go home, Ted. Find yourself another monkey!

(DOREEN *returns. A long pause.* BOB *has his back to* TED *and won't turn round.* TED *tries to say something—to patch it up—make a joke—anything—but nothing comes. He gives it up and with a sudden rough gesture walks past* DOREEN *and slams out of the room.*)

DOREEN. Where's he going?

BOB. Home.

DOREEN. Home?

BOB. Yes.

DOREEN. You mean he's not coming back?

BOB. I don't think so, no.

DOREEN (*Unable to take it in*). You mean he's just gone off like that without even saying goodnight?

BOB. Well, yes . . . He had work to do at home, very urgent. Remember, he did say.

DOREEN. Did he?

BOB. Yes. And he won't let anything stand in the way of his work. That's what's called drive.

DOREEN. Have you two had words, then?

BOB. No.

DOREEN. What about?

BOB. Nothing.

DOREEN. Was it about me?

BOB. Of course not! Why should it be?

DOREEN. I don't know I'm sure. (*She goes to the door, opens it, and disappears onto the landing.*)

BOB. Here—drink your coffee. It's getting cold.

DOREEN (*Returning*). I think that's the rudest thing I ever heard of. Ever, in my whole life.

BOB. He didn't mean it that way.

DOREEN. Well, what way did he mean it then?

BOB. Oh hell, I don't know. Drink your coffee.

DOREEN. I don't want it.

BOB. Then leave it! . . . I'm sorry.

DOREEN. Don't mention it.

BOB. It's my fault really.

DOREEN. Why?

BOB. I've had too much to drink. I can't carry it. Alcohol's not really a stimulant at all, you know—it's a depressant.

DOREEN. I know. I heard.

BOB (*Smiling*). He means well, you know. He really does. You can't hold things against him.

DOREEN. Why not?

BOB. Because that's the way he is. He's like that in the office—offhand, always joking . . .

DOREEN. Yes. I bet he'll have a joke about me tomorrow.

BOB. Of course not.

DOREEN. I bet . . . What office would that be, anyway?

BOB. I told you. Export-import.

DOREEN. No, I mean the actual address.

BOB. The address? What for?

DOREEN. Nothing. I just asked. It must be nice having someone in the office. Someone you're close to.

BOB. We're not close.

DOREEN. I thought you were friends.

BOB (*Passionately*). Well, we're obviously not! Why should we be? We only work in the same office—we've nothing in common. He comes into work, and he's glad to be there. I hate it. Some mornings I can hardly get out of that bed for thinking how I'm going to spend the day. When I wake up I've got so much energy. I could write a whole book—paint great swirling pictures on the ceiling. But what am I *actually* going to do? Just fill in about five hundred invoices.

DOREEN. Well, that's life, isn't it?

BOB. Look. You're a typist. Are you going to spend the rest of your life being somebody else's obedient servant, original and two carbons?

DOREEN. Well, like I say, we haven't got much choice, have we?

BOB. Yes we have. We must have. We weren't born to do this. Eyes. Complicated things like eyes, weren't made by God just to see columns of pounds, shillings, and pence written up in a ledger. Tongues! Good grief, the woman next to me in the office even sounds like a typewriter. A thin, chipped old typewriter. Do you know how many thousands of years it took to make anything so beautiful, so feeling, as your hand? People say I know something like the back of my hand, but they don't know their hands. They wouldn't recognize a photograph of them. Why? Because their hands are anonymous. They're just tools for filing invoices, turning lathes around. They cramp up from picking slag out of moving belts of coal. If that's not blasphemy, what is?

(*A tiny pause.*)

DOREEN. What's the time?

BOB. Half past.

DOREEN. Well, I really must be going now. (*She gets up and goes for her coat.*)

BOB (*Urgently*). You're quite pretty, you know.

DOREEN. Thanks.

BOB. I mean, very pretty really. (*He helps her put on the coat.*) You know, I always thought an ocelot was a bird.

DOREEN. Did you?

BOB. Yes. I must have been thinking of an ostrich.

DOREEN. I'll let you into a secret. It's not really ocelot.

BOB. Isn't it?

DOREEN. No, it's only nylon. It's not really cold enough for fur coats, anyway, is it? I was just showing off.

BOB. I'm glad you were. I'll let *you* into a secret.

DOREEN. What?

BOB. Some nights when I come back here I give Behemoth a record for his supper. That's the way I look at him sometimes, feeding off records, you know. And I conduct it. If it's a concerto I play the solo part, running up and down the keyboard, doing the expressive bits, everything. I imagine someone I love is sitting out in the audience watching; you know, someone I want to admire me . . . Anyway, it sort of frees things inside me. At great moments I feel shivery all over. It's marvelous to feel shivery like that. What I want to know is—why can't I feel like that in my work? There's something inside me that can be excited. And that means I could excite other people, if I only knew what way . . . I never met anyone to show me that way.

DOREEN. Well, I really must be going now.

BOB. How about one more record before you go? . . . One for
the road, as they say. Something more tuneful and luscious?
Madame Butterfly? D'you know the Love Duet? You'll like
that. I know it's awfully corny, but I do love all that fudgy
sort of music. At least I have great sort of craving for it.
Like I suppose some people have for chocolates. Try a bit.

DOREEN. Well really, it is getting rather late.

BOB (*Desperately*). It only takes three minutes.

(*Pause.*)

DOREEN (*Reluctantly*). All right.

(*He puts on the record, not looking at her. We hear the
quiet orchestral music before Butterfly begins to sing
"Vogliatemi bene, un bene piccolino."*)

BOB. You know what's happening, don't you? Pinkerton—that's
the American sailor—has married this Japanese girl in
spite of her family and the priests and everybody. And this
is the first time they're alone together . . .

(*There now follows a six minute sequence in which not a
word is spoken.*)
*At first both stand—he by the gramophone, she by the
door—in attitudes of strain. Then the warmth of the music
gives* BOB *the courage to gesture her towards the armchair,
and she tiptoes across the room and sits in it.*
*She listens for a moment, and finds it surprisingly pleas-
ant. She smiles. He sits on the stool near the table, then sur-
reptitiously edges it nearer to her. He reaches out his hand to
touch the ocelot coat: she notices this, and the boy hastily
mimes a gesture to indicate smoking. She nods. He rises*

[55]

eagerly, and gets her the cigarettes: in his nervousness he opens the box of matches upside down, and they scatter all over the floor. They pick them up together. Finally, kneeling, he lights her cigarette—then, fascinated by her prettiness, he stares up at her. The flame of the match burns between them until she gently blows it out.

She offers him a puff: he declines—then accepts. He inhales and chokes a little. He takes her hand and begins to study it with intense concentration. The music increases in ardor.

Suddenly DOREEN *is sorry for him. She closes her eyes and lowers her face to be kissed. Lightly, hardly daring, he responds by kissing her forehead. She opens her eyes a little impatiently, and tugs at her ocelot coat: it is rather hot, isn't it? With clumsy fingers he helps her out of it, and she makes herself more comfortable, tucking her legs under her in the chair. Then again she closes her eyes and invites his kiss.*

This time he touches her lips. Clumsily, hardly knowing what to do, his arms grope for her body. The eagerness of his response surprises and alarms the girl. She begins to struggle as the boy's excitement grows. Their positions in the chair becoming increasingly ridiculous, as she seeks to avoid his embrace with her legs trapped under her. Above them the voices of the operatic lovers sing ecstatically of love. Finally, DOREEN *struggles free:* BOB *is left lying in an absurd position across the armchair.*

He stands up, rumpled and upset. He is no longer listening to the inhuman, undisturbable lovers: he is desperate. Slowly, his mind full of how TED *would act under these circumstances, he begins pursuing her: as slowly, she retreats to the corner of the room, and stumbles back on to the bed. The boy falls softly on top of her, and tries with a deep muddled gentleness to show her passion. She tries haplessly to avoid him. Finally she half rises and pushes him to the floor. Then she gets up, adjusts her clothes, and moves away from him across the room.*

BOB *stares at her. Then he, too, gets up, and comes towards her with a gesture at once desperate and supplicating. Puccini's Love Duet rises to its climax. As the final, unifying chord of deliciousness crashes over the room,* DOREEN *slaps the boy's face—then, horrified, takes it between her hands, trying to recall the blow. Slowly* BOB *backs away from her across the width of the room. The music dies away; the record turns itself off. Silence hangs between them.* BOB *speaks at last.*

BOB. I'm sorry.

DOREEN. That's all right.

BOB. No, no, it isn't. It isn't at all. Actually, you see, I've brought you here under false pretenses.

DOREEN. What d'you mean?

BOB. I've got a girl friend of my own already.

DOREEN. You have?

BOB. Yes.

DOREEN. Is that her? (*She indicates the photograph of the girl left by* TED *in the corner of the mirror. A pause.*)

BOB. Yes.

DOREEN. Can I see?

(*He passes it to her.*)

She looks lovely.

BOB. Yes, she is. Very. That's really raven black, her hair. It's got tints of blue in it. You can't really judge from a photo.

DOREEN. What's her name?

BOB. Er . . . Lavinia. It's rather an unusual name, isn't it? Lavinia. I think it's rather distinguished.

DOREEN. Yes, it is.

BOB. Like her. She's distinguished. She's got a way with her. Style, you know. It's what they used to call "carriage."

(*She gives him a startled look.*)

We're going to get married.

DOREEN. When?

BOB. Very soon. So you see it wasn't right of me to bring you here. Anyway, no harm done, I suppose.

DOREEN. No, of course not. (*They go to the door.*) Well, it's been lovely. I enjoyed the music. Really.

BOB. Did you?

DOREEN. Perhaps we'll meet again. At a concert or somewhere.

BOB. Yes.

DOREEN. I'm glad about your girl. She looks lovely.

BOB (*Almost out of control*). She is.

(*He opens the door and lets her out.*)

Fabian and Carter.

DOREEN. Pardon?

BOB. The name of the firm where TED works. You wanted to know it. Fabian and Carter. Bishopsgate 2437. Goodbye.

DOREEN. Goodbye.

(*She gives him a quick smile and goes. He shuts the door. He turns and surveys the empty room. Then he walks almost aimlessly across it.*

He stops by the gramophone. He puts it on. We hear the first strains of Madame Butterfly. He stands by it as it plays. He looks down at the record turning. He kneels to it, stretching out his arms to enfold it.

Suddenly he draws his hands back. He takes off the pick-up, and, with a vicious gesture, scratches the record twice, damaging it beyond repair.

A pause. The boy replaces the pick-up. Again the Love Duet fills the shabby room, but now there is a deep scratch clicking through it, ruining it.

The stage darkens.

BOB *stands rigid beside Behemoth.*

SLOW CURTAIN

THE
PUBLIC
EYE
A Comedy in One Act

Characters

JULIAN CRISTOFOROU

CHARLES SIDLEY

BELINDA SIDLEY

The curtain rises on the outer office of CHARLES SIDLEY, *Chartered Accountant, in Bloomsbury. It is a well-furnished room in white, gold and russet, with many white bookshelves laden with works of reference. There is a desk where a secretary customarily sits, a sofa, and two doors. One leads out into the hall of the building, the other into* CHARLES' *office and is marked:* PRIVATE.

When the door is open we can see stairs going up to higher floors.

It is mid-morning, and sunlight streams brightly through a large window.

On a chair sits JULIAN CRISTOFOROU, *studying a large turnip watch. He is a man in his middle thirties; his whole air breathes a gentle eccentricity, a nervousness combined with an air of almost meek self-disapprobation and a certain bright detachment. He is bundled in a white raincoat, with many pockets. Sighing, he drops the watch into a large leather bag, like a Gladstone, which is beside him. Then he reaches into one pocket and extracts a large handkerchief, which he spreads over his knees; from another he produces a packet of raisins and pours them out; from a third, a packet of nuts, and does likewise. He just begins to eat them when he cocks his ear, hastily stuffs the handkerchief away in a fourth pocket and sits upright and unconcerned as the inner door opens and* CHARLES SIDLEY *comes out.*

CHARLES *is a good-looking man of forty, exact and almost finicky in his speech, with a fairly steady line in pompous sarcasm, and another, more immediately concealed, in self-pity.*

JULIAN. Good morning.

CHARLES (*Surprised to see him*). Good morning.

JULIAN. Mr. Sidley?

CHARLES. Correct.

JULIAN. I'm delighted.

CHARLES. You want to see me?

JULIAN. It's rather more that I have to. Not that I don't want to see you, of course.

CHARLES. Well, I'm sorry, but I was just on my way home. The office isn't really open on Saturday mornings; I was just doing a little work.

JULIAN. I know. I saw you.

CHARLES. I beg your pardon?

JULIAN. I peeped into your office before. But you were so engrossed I didn't like to disturb you.

CHARLES. How long have you been waiting, then?

JULIAN. About half an hour.

CHARLES. Half—

JULIAN. Oh, please don't apologize. It's a positive joy to wait in a room like this. There are so many delights to detain one. Your reference books, for instance. Overwhelming!

CHARLES. Thank you.

JULIAN. I perceive you have a passion for accuracy.

CHARLES. Let's say a respect for fact.

JULIAN. Oh, let's indeed. I do admire that. And in an accountant a first essential, surely. Mind you, one must be careful. Facts can become an obsession. I hope they aren't with you.

CHARLES. I hope so, too. Now, if you don't mind—perhaps I can make an appointment for next week.

JULIAN (*Ignoring him, staring at the shelves*). Websters! Chambers! Whittakers Almanac! Even the names have a certain leathery beauty. And how imposing they look on shelves. Serried ranks of learning!

CHARLES (*Brutally*). Are you a salesman?

JULIAN. Forgive me. I was lapsing. Yes, I was once. But then I was everything once. I had twenty-three positions before I was thirty.

CHARLES. Did you really?

JULIAN. I know what you're thinking. A striking record of failure. But you're wrong. I never fail in jobs, they fail me.

CHARLES. Well, I really must be getting home now. I'm sorry to have kept you waiting, even inadvertently. May I make an appointment for you early next week?

JULIAN. Certainly. If that's what you want.

CHARLES. Well, as I say, I don't receive clients at the weekend. Now let me look at my secretary's book . . . What about next Tuesday?

JULIAN (*Considering*). I don't really like Tuesdays. They're an indeterminate sort of day.

CHARLES (*With a touch of exasperation*). Well you name it Mr.—

JULIAN. Cristoforou.

CHARLES. Cristoforou?

JULIAN. Yes. With an "f," not a "ph." It's a little downbeat, I admit. Balkan cigarettes and conspirator mustaches. I don't care for it, but it's not to be avoided. My father was a Rhodes Scholar. I mean he was a scholar from Rhodes.

CHARLES (*With desperate politeness*). Oh yes?

JULIAN. Why don't you call me Julian? That's a good between-the-wars name. Cricket pads and a secret passion for E. M. Forster. That's my mother's influence. She had connections with Bloomsbury. To be precise, a boarding house.

CHARLES. Would you please tell me when you would like to see me?

JULIAN. It's rather more when *you* would like, isn't it?

CHARLES. I have no special relationship with the days of the week, Mr. Cristoforou.

JULIAN. Oh no more have I, in the final analysis. I mean they don't actually prevent me from doing things on them. They merely encourage or discourage.

CHARLES. I suppose I could squeeze you in late on Monday if it's urgent.

JULIAN. I had imagined it was. In fact, I must admit to feeling disappointed.

CHARLES. I'm sorry—

JULIAN. No, if the truth be known, extremely surprised.

CHARLES. Surprised?

JULIAN. At your being so off-hand. I had imagined you differently.

CHARLES. Are you in some kind of trouble?

JULIAN. Your trouble is mine, sir. It's one of my mottoes. Not inappropriate, I think. Still, of course, I mustn't be unreasonable. It's your decision. After all, you're paying.

CHARLES. I'm what?

JULIAN. Paying. (*He pretends to go out.*)

CHARLES. Mr. Cristoforou, come here. I had assumed you were here to see me professionally.

JULIAN. Certainly.

CHARLES. Well?

JULIAN. Well it's more you wishing to see me, isn't it? Or hear from me anyway.

CHARLES. Perhaps you'd better state your business with me very precisely.

JULIAN. You mean to say you don't know what it is?

CHARLES. How can I?

JULIAN. You don't know why I'm here?

CHARLES. I haven't the faintest idea.

JULIAN. How appalling. I'm agonized. I'm really agonized! What must you think of me? Chattering away and you not even knowing why I'm here. Well of course I'd assumed—but then you shouldn't assume anything. Certainly not in my business. I'm afraid it's absolutely typical of me. My wits are scattered when they should be most collected. You haven't got a spoon on you by any chance?

CHARLES. A spoon?

JULIAN. For my yoghurt. Forgive me, it's a distressing symptom of nervousness which I've never been able to conquer. I always eat when I'm embarrassed. Or, as in this case, agonized. (*He takes out a carton of yoghurt from his pocket.*)

CHARLES. Mr. Cristoforou, I'm not noted for my patient disposition.

JULIAN. I'm glad to hear that. Patience too long controlled turns to cruelty. That's an old Persian proverb. At least I think it's Persian. It could be Hindu. Do you have a dictionary of proverbs?

CHARLES (*Bluntly*). Who are you?

JULIAN. I'm Parkinson's replacement.

CHARLES. Replacement?

JULIAN. From Mayhew and Figgis. Now there are two names which are quite inappropriate for a Detective Agency. They should be snuffmakers to the Duke of Cumberland or something like that. Don't you agree?

CHARLES. Are you telling me that you are employed by Mayhew and Figgis as a private detective?

JULIAN (*Producing a china cannister labelled sugar, and attempting to pour some on his yoghurt*). Of course. What else? I'm here to make our monthly report. The office was to telephone you and say I'd be coming today. They obviously failed. Very embarrassing. For both of us.

(*Referring to the cannister.*)

That's empty.

CHARLES. And you are here in place of Parkinson?

JULIAN. Exactly.

CHARLES. Why? Where is he?

JULIAN. He's not with us any more.

CHARLES. You mean he resigned?

JULIAN. No. He was thrown down an elevator shaft in Goodge Street. Do you know it? It's just off the Tottenham Court Road—

CHARLES. I know where it is.

JULIAN. Hazards of the game, you know. No one mourns him more than I.

(*He opens the desk drawer and extracts a spoon.*)

When there's a secretary, there's always a teaspoon.

(*Grimly,* CHARLES *dials.*)

CHARLES. Hello? Mayhew and Figgis? This is Mr. Sidley. Mr. Charles Sidley. I'd like to speak to Mr. Mayhew. If he's not there I should like his home number. Yes. Good. Thank you. (*Irritably.*) Hello? Mr. Mayhew? Mr. Sidley here. I have a man in my office at this moment calling himself Cristoforou. He claims to be an employee of yours. What? . . . Yes? . . . Oh. Oh, I see Yes, he told me that. Goodge Street. Yes, *I know where it is!* Very regrettable. A most efficient man.

(*Looking at* JULIAN.)

(*Surprised.*) He is? Well I hope I can, Mr. Mayhew, I hope I can. This is a very delicate matter, as you know. What? No, of course I understand that: yours is a firm of the very highest—Yes, I say I know: yours is a firm of the very highest—Yes, yes, of course: I realize that. Naturally. Yours is a firm of the very highest—(*Pause.*) Well, we'll see, Mr. Mayhew. I am always willing to give people the benefit of the doubt, though I may add that when I say doubt in this case, I mean doubt. Good morning. (*He hangs up*). You have a garrulous employer.

JULIAN. Only where he feels his honor to be at stake. After all, his is a firm of the very highest. (*He smiles his bright smile.* CHARLES *glares.*) In this case he said I'd been with it for three years and did the most expert work. Yes?

CHARLES. Correct, as it happens.

JULIAN. Well, it happens to be true. At the risk of sounding forward, I am a superb detective. It's one of the few jobs where being nondescript is an advantage.

(*He takes off his raincoat to reveal an astounding striped suit underneath.*)

CHARLES. One would hardly describe you as nondescript, Mr. Cristoforou.

JULIAN. Oh yes. I attained nondescript a long time ago. Last year I became characterless. This year, superfluous. Next year I shall be invisible. It's rather like one of those

American Gain Confidence Courses in reverse. Make Nothing of Yourself in Six Easy Lessons! . . . Actually I've been working on your affair for four weeks. Mayhew's is a large agency, and we often take over each other's assignments. It's quite routine.

CHARLES. All the same, a little highhanded, I'd say.

JULIAN. I'm sorry you'd say that.

CHARLES. In any case, how did you know I was here?

JULIAN. I am a detective, Mr. Sidley. You work here every Saturday morning, and your wife goes to the Cordon Bleu for a cooking lesson.

CHARLES. Correct.

JULIAN. It was an obvious opportunity to come around.

CHARLES. I see. Very thorough I'm sure. Now perhaps you would oblige me by reading your report.

JULIAN. Of course. That's why I'm here.

CHARLES. One would never know it.

(JULIAN *sits down and gropes in the Gladstone bag. He struggles with it for a moment and produces not the report, but an immense plastic bag of macaroons.*)

JULIAN. Would you like a macaroon? Excuse me. It's really disgusting this eating business, I know. I have a friend who's a lawyer, and he gets so nervous about speaking in court, he eats sweets all day long. In his last murder case he devoured twenty-six Mars Bars in a morning. You're not a lawyer, are you?

CHARLES. No.

JULIAN. Of course not; an accountant. Silly of me. Scattered wits again! That's almost like being a priest today, isn't it? I mean, people do what you tell them without question.

(*He takes out his report.*)

What did poor Parkinson tell you at your last meeting?

CHARLES. Surely you know that already, if you inherited his assignment.

JULIAN. His report was negative.

CHARLES. Correct.

JULIAN. Your suspicions were unfounded.

CHARLES. So he said. The point is, are they still? A month has gone by since then.

JULIAN. That rather depends on what they were, doesn't it?

CHARLES. You know very well what they were. What they always are when you call in a detective. Are you trying to be humorous?

JULIAN. I sometimes succeed in being humorous, Mr. Sidley, but I never try. Suspicion is a highly subjective word. It refers with exactitude only to the man who entertains it.

CHARLES. Mr. Cristoforou, what do I have to do to get from you the information I am paying for?

JULIAN (*Reasonably*). I don't know what that is, Mr. Sidley. If you wish to know whether your wife is being sexually unfaithful to you, I must point out that it is extremely difficult for a private eye to witness copulation.

CHARLES. How dare you?

JULIAN. It's even more difficult to witness the *desire* for copulation. Inevitably, therefore, there is no proof that your wife has slept outside her marriage bed.

CHARLES. No proof.

JULIAN. None whatever.

CHARLES. Then you have nothing to tell me.

JULIAN. I wouldn't say that.

CHARLES. Then what would you say? In a word, what— would—you—say?

JULIAN. I haven't got a word.

CHARLES. Then find one.

JULIAN (*Hastily*). Perhaps I'd better read my report. (*The* DETECTIVE *picks up his report and tries to open it. Unfortunately the pages seem to be gummed together.*) Oh dear. That's syrup.

CHARLES. What?

JULIAN. I tried to transport a waffle yesterday.

(*He tries for a long moment to separate the pages of his report. It tears badly. He looks at his employer with hapless eyes.* CHARLES *stares back in a thunderous silence.*)

(*Ingratiatingly.*) Well, I can read the first page anyway. (JULIAN *picks up the first page, which is in two bits, and reads in an official voice.*) "Report by J. Cristoforou on the movements of Mrs. Charles Sidley. Wednesday: September 22nd."

CHARLES. Never mind about that.

JULIAN. That was my first day, you see.

CHARLES. Go on.

JULIAN. "10:48 subject leaves house. Takes taxi at corner of Walton and Pont Street." That's always a tricky one, by the way. Have you ever considered what one does if one's quarry hails a taxi and there isn't another in sight?

CHARLES. I'd always assumed you drove a car.

JULIAN. Ah, sadly, no longer. I used to be the ace driver of the agency, but one day I was shadowing a man I suspected of trading secrets with an enemy power. He was on foot, his umbrella stuffed with miles of stolen microfilm. I was in my car—a minute Morris in a discreet shade of daffodil. Suddenly he darted through the main door of Westminster Abbey. I had no choice but to follow him.

CHARLES. In your minute car?

JULIAN. Certainly. If I was to catch him in the act, there was obviously no time to lose.

CHARLES. What happened?

JULIAN. I crashed into the baptismal font and completely ruined a royal christening. As a result they took away my license. Very vindictive, I thought, considering I was acting in the national interest.

CHARLES. You drove a car into Westminster Abbey?

JULIAN. Yes. Do you know it? It's in Parliament Square.

CHARLES. I KNOW WHERE IT IS! Continue, please.

JULIAN. "Subject proceeds to Madame Martha, hatmaker, of 32 Marble Street."

CHARLES. Could you see in?

JULIAN. Yes.

CHARLES. Who was there?

JULIAN. Four old ladies.

CHARLES. Any men?

JULIAN. I don't think so.

CHARLES. You don't think?

JULIAN. I mean they may have been dressed as ladies. It's just a possibility in a hat shop.

CHARLES. I see.

JULIAN. "Subject collects hat, which appears to be already ordered, and emerges, wearing it. Hat resembles a wilted lettuce."

CHARLES. Watch what you say, please. Everything my wife knows about hats, or clothes of any kind, she learned from me. When I first met her she wore nothing but sweaters and trousers. When you criticize her taste in hats, you are criticizing me.

JULIAN. I'm terribly sorry.

CHARLES. I suppose it's only natural that now she's moved away from me she should revert to type. All this last week she's worn nothing but a hideous green little trilby.

JULIAN. You don't like it?

CHARLES. You do?

JULIAN. I think it has a certain gamin chic.

CHARLES. Continue, please.

JULIAN. "11:30 subject in exquisite green hat walks up Brompton Road, enters the Michaelangelo Coffee Bar. Orders a Leaning Tower of Pisa."

CHARLES. What the hell's that?

JULIAN. A phallic confection of tutti frutti, chocolate chips, nougat, stem ginger, toasted almonds and molasses—the whole cloud capped with cream . . . It goes on, and on . . . Your wife is rather partial to it. So, as a matter of irrelevant fact, am I. Do you have a sweet tooth?

CHARLES. Never mind about my teeth. What happened next?

JULIAN. "12:17 subject rises and goes into Kensington Gardens. Walks to the statue of Peter Pan." Do you believe in fairies?

CHARLES. What did she do?

JULIAN. She looked at it and laughed. A curious reaction, I thought.

CHARLES. Not at all. The first week we were married I showed her that statue and explained to her precisely why it was ridiculous. When you criticize her taste in statuary you criticize me.

JULIAN. Please forgive me. I don't know where to look.

CHARLES. At your report.

JULIAN. Yes . . . Certainly . . .

CHARLES. She was waiting for someone, I presume.

JULIAN. On the contrary, she wandered about quite aimlessly.

CHARLES. How do you know it was aimlessly?

JULIAN. At one point she picked up some acorns.

CHARLES. Acorns?

JULIAN. Yes; to throw at the ducks. I got the impression she had nothing better to do.

CHARLES. Charming! That's the result of all my work, trying to teach her to spend her leisure properly.

JULIAN. It was a very nice day.

CHARLES. What's that got to do with it?

JULIAN. I was trying to be indulgent.

CHARLES. You're not paid for indulgence, are you?

JULIAN. No.

CHARLES. Then get on.

JULIAN. Yes. "12:55 subject leaves park and enters a cinema in Oxford Street. It was showing the film 'I was A Teenage Necrophile.'"

CHARLES. Did you go in after her?

JULIAN. Naturally.

CHARLES. And she sat by herself?

JULIAN. Throughout. Four hours and seventeen minutes.

CHARLES. Four hours . . . ?

JULIAN. She saw it twice.

CHARLES. What did you make of that?

JULIAN. I thought it argued the most amazing capacity to suspend disbelief.

CHARLES. Indeed.

JULIAN. It was a very tasteless film. But worse ones were to follow. I mean on subsequent days.

CHARLES. And that was how she spent her day?

JULIAN. Yes.

CHARLES. After all I've taught her. How dare she? . . . How dare she??! . . . (*Upset.*) I beg your pardon. It's not an easy thing to set detectives on your wife. It must seem rather bad form to you—or it would if,—well.

JULIAN. If I wasn't one myself. It still does, Mr. Sidley. I must admit I end up despising many of our clients.

CHARLES. Despising? That's rather rich coming from you, isn't it?

JULIAN. Oh yes, I daresay. It's something of a reflex action. They despise me, after all.

CHARLES. What else do you expect?

JULIAN. Nothing. The client looks down on the whore who relieves him. It's a familiar pattern.

CHARLES. Charming image.

JULIAN. But not inappropriate, I think.

CHARLES. If you think like that, why do you do it?

JULIAN. Private reasons. Or, to be exact, public reasons.

CHARLES. I don't understand.

JULIAN. It's not important. At the risk of being impertinent, Mr. Sidley, why did you come to us? You really had nothing to go on.

CHARLES. You mean nothing concrete. No letters written in a hot impetuous hand. No guilty smiles or blushes. My dear man, we live in the twentieth century, which blushes at nothing. The blush has gone out, like the ball-card and the billet-doux. Betrayal has become a word with rather quaint connotations.

JULIAN. I think that's just rhetoric, Mr. Sidley. Rather well managed, if I may say so, but not true at all.

CHARLES. No? My wife has no more conception of sexual fidelity than that chair. When I married her, she thought nothing of sleeping with three different men in the same week.

JULIAN. Was one of them you?

CHARLES. I don't think I need to answer that.

JULIAN. Oh come. If you're like a priest in your profession, I'm like a psychoanalyst in mine. You can't afford to withhold information. Unlike an analyst, I'm not considered a gentleman, so you can tell me everything. If this was true, why did you marry her?

CHARLES. Because . . . I was infatuated with her.

(A pause. CHARLES almost visibly unbends a little.)

JULIAN. Continue, please.

CHARLES. I don't see what possible bearing this could have on the situation.

JULIAN. Oh! But you must let me be the judge of that. Where did you meet her?

CHARLES. In a place called the Up-to-Date Club in Soho.

JULIAN. It doesn't seem the sort of place you would go to.

CHARLES. I was taken there by a journalist friend. I must say it was very pleasant. It had a dining room upstairs with French cooking and a sort of cellar below where you could dance. I wasn't very good at dancing—at least not all that jungle warfare they call dancing—but the food was delicious, and Belinda served it.

JULIAN. Belinda?

CHARLES. My wife. She didn't serve it very well either; she was always forgetting one's order and having to come back for it—which I found more agreeable than otherwise . . . I caught myself going there rather often. Finally I asked her out to a theatre. She'd never seen anything more complicated in her life than a horror film. She was absolutely obsessed by horror films.

JULIAN. She still is.

CHARLES. Yes . . . It was a curious courtship. Without my demanding it, of course, she surrendered her whole life to me, for remaking. In a way, I suppose it wasn't too surprising. She'd lived in Northampton for the first eighteen years, and that's enough to smother anybody. Her father was in shoes. Her parents' ambitions for her extended no further than a job at the library and marriage with a local boy. Very properly she ran away to London, where she led the most extraordinary life, sharing a flat with two artists, one of whom baked his canvasses in an oven, whilst

the other spat paint onto his direct from his mouth—
thereby expressing contempt for society, I believe. It's not
surprising really, since at the time she was comparing them
both to El Greco, that she reacted to some tactful reform
with enthusiasm. For my part, I taught her everything I
could. I'm not an expert, Mr. Cristoforou: I'm that old-
fashioned, but I hope not too comical thing, a dilettante.
Of course the notion of an accountant with what, in the
days when Europe was the world, used to be called a soul,
probably strikes you as ludicrous. I'm afraid there's a
great deal about this situation which is ludicrous. The
moral, of course, is that men of forty shouldn't marry girls
of eighteen. It should be a law of the church like con-
sanguinity: only marry in your generation. And yet it
began so well . . .

JULIAN. You were happy?

CHARLES. Deeply. She renewed my life. I had someone to share
things with: show things to.

JULIAN. And she? Did she show things to you?

CHARLES. She didn't need to. She was young and that was
enough. Youth needs only to show itself. It's like the sun
in that respect. In company with many men of my age, I
found I was slipping away into middle life, journeying, as
it were, into a colder latitude. I didn't like it. I didn't like
it at all.

JULIAN. So you went after the sun. Tried to bottle a ray or two.

CHARLES. Foolish, imbecile attempt. Within a year I had to
recognize that I had married a child. Someone with no
sense of her place at all.

[81]

JULIAN. Her place?

CHARLES. Certainly. Her place. Belinda is the wife of a professional man in a highly organized city in the twentieth century. That is her place. As I have often explained to her, this would undoubtedly be different if she were wedded to a jazz trumpeter in New Orleans, which she seems to think she is. There is no such thing as a perfectly independent person.

JULIAN. Is that what she wants to be?

CHARLES (*Irritably*). I don't know what she wants to be. She doesn't know herself. Things have got steadily worse. Three months ago I invited a very important client to dinner, the President of one of the largest investment companies in the City. My wife presided over my table dressed in what I can only describe as a leather pajama suit. When I remonstrated with her, she said she was sick of stuffy guests.

JULIAN. It's a fair point.

CHARLES (*Hotly*). It's not a fair point. (*Exasperated*). My friends are not stuffy, Mr. Cristoforou, just because they don't come to dinner disguised as motor cyclists. No doubt they are helplessly out of touch with modern living. They only read, think, travel, and exchange the fruits of doing so pleasurably with each other. Is there anything so utterly boring and ridiculous as the modern worship of youth?

JULIAN. Nothing, no. It's like sun worship. Debasing and superstitious.

CHARLES (*Looking at him suspiciously*). No doubt this is very amusing to you.

JULIAN. How can you think that?

CHARLES. You think it's sour grapes?

JULIAN. Of course not!

CHARLES. Oh yes!

JULIAN. Mr. Sidley, I beg you—

CHARLES (*With real pain*). Has my wife a lover?

JULIAN. What makes you think she has?

CHARLES (*In a defeated voice*). Because for three months now she has turned away from me. Just turned away. You know how women avert their faces when they don't want to be kissed. Well, she is averting her face, her look, her mind. Everything. Whole meals go by in silence, and when she talks, she appears not to be listening to what she herself is saying. In the old days she used to stay in bed until long after I'd gone to the office. I used to remonstrate with her about it. Now she's up and out of the house sometimes before eight. As if she can't bear to lie in my bed another minute. . . . Last week one morning she was up at six. When I asked her where she was going, she said she wanted to watch the sun come up on Hampstead Heath.

(*Explosively.*)

God damn it, d'you think I'm a fool? She's seeing someone else, isn't she? Look—last night she didn't come in at all!

JULIAN. At all?

CHARLES. Well, not until well past two. And not one word of explanation.

JULIAN. Did you ask her for one?

CHARLES. If I ask her for anything, that's a quarrel in a minute. (*Pause.*) Tell me. There's someone else, isn't there?

JULIAN (*Quietly*). Yes.

CHARLES. Go on.

JULIAN. I find this hard.

CHARLES. Go on. How often do they meet?

JULIAN. Every day.

CHARLES. Every day?

JULIAN. Yes.

CHARLES. Describe him.

JULIAN. Well . . . he's handsome, I'd say.

CHARLES (*Bitterly*). Of course.

JULIAN. Full of a kind of confidence: you know—debonair, well-dressed. I'd say he was a diplomat.

CHARLES. A diplomat? . . . There was that party at the Nicaraguan Embassy.

JULIAN. No, he's definitely not Nicaraguan.

CHARLES. How do you know that?

JULIAN. Ah! That's a very fair point. You have an acute mind, Mr. Sidley. I admit that when you meet a complete stranger for the first time there is no definite way of knowing he's not Nicaraguan.

CHARLES. How does he behave to her?

JULIAN. With great politeness. He shows a most striking restraint.

CHARLES. You mean they don't actually kiss in public?

JULIAN. Certainly not!

CHARLES. What *do* they do, then?

JULIAN. Oh . . . stare at each other happily. Exchange looks of deep meaning. Give those little secret smiles—you know— I think the French call them "oeillades." I'm sure that's the word. Shall I look it up?

CHARLES. Secret smiles . . .

JULIAN. I'd say, watching from a distance, their relationship was one of the utmost tenderness.

CHARLES. Would you?

JULIAN. Yes I would.

CHARLES. Damn her!

JULIAN. Mr. Sidley—

CHARLES. Damn her! Damn her!! (*Furiously.*) What's his name?

JULIAN. I don't know.

CHARLES. Where does he live?

JULIAN. I don't know.

CHARLES. Liar!

JULIAN. I don't.

CHARLES. (*Grabbing him*). Listen to me. You're a private detective, aren't you?

JULIAN. You know I am.

CHARLES. And it's your job to find out names and addresses?

JULIAN. I suppose it is.

CHARLES (*Shaking him*). Well you find out this man's name and address by tonight, or I'll break your bloody neck! (*He hurls him down on to the sofa.*)

JULIAN. Mr. Sidley! You've no right to handle me like this. I'm a professional man.

CHARLES. You're a sneaking, prying, impertinent little reptile!

JULIAN. I didn't want to tell you. You made me. Be honest. You made me.

BELINDA (*Off*). Charles!

CHARLES. Be quiet!

BELINDA (*Off*). Charles!

CHARLES (*Amazed*). It's my wife! (*He crosses to left door, opens it and looks out; then closes and locks it.*) She's coming upstairs. What am I going to do? You must get out of here.

JULIAN. How can I?

CHARLES. Through here. (*Unlocking right door.*) Down the fire escape and into the mews. Quick! Telephone me at home in an hour. Hurry!

JULIAN. What's your number?

CHARLES. I'm in the book.

JULIAN. Right! (*He dashes out through* CHARLES' *private office.*)

CHARLES (*Loudly*). Coming, dear.

JULIAN (*Returning*). Hey!

CHARLES (*Whispering*). What?

JULIAN. My macaroons!

CHARLES. PLEASE! . . .

(CRISTOFOROU *grabs his macaroons and runs out.* CHARLES *slams the door on him, wipes his brow, then unlocks the other door.* BELINDA *appears, carrying an enormous armful of flowers. She is a pretty young girl of twenty-two, wearing bright unconventional clothes and a green trilby.*)

Hello, dear. This is an unexpected pleasure!

BELINDA (*Entering*). Why is the door locked?

CHARLES. I always keep it locked on Saturday mornings. You know I don't receive clients at the weekend. Why aren't you at your Cordon Bleu?

BELINDA. I got tired of learning the right way to hold a saucepan; so I left.

CHARLES. And came here?

BELINDA. Obviously.

CHARLES. Why? You haven't been here in over a year.

BELINDA. I was just passing.

CHARLES. Passing?

BELINDA. Yes. I thought I'd collect you. Surprise, lovely surprise.

(*Seeing the carton left by mistake on the desk.*)

[87]

Who eats yogurt?

CHARLES. I do.

BELINDA. Since when? I thought you loathed it.

CHARLES (*Picking it up*). Did you? Aha! Well you don't know everything about me.

BELINDA. I'll order some at home.

CHARLES (*Tasting it*). No thank you.

BELINDA. Why not? If you like it.

CHARLES (*Testily*). I like it in the office. I do not like it at home. It's as simple as that.

BELINDA. Are you feeling all right?

CHARLES. Perfectly.

BELINDA. Well you don't look it. (*She dumps flowers into the vase.*)

CHARLES. Belinda, this is only my office.

BELINDA. I know where it is, Charles, and it needs them. Aren't they lovely? There was a man at the corner selling them off a barrow. I think he was a Malayan. At any rate he had topaz eyes, so I bought the lot. Two pounds ten with the greenery. The Malayan said if I bought everything there'd be no monsoon over my temple for a year. Wasn't that a sweet thing to say?

CHARLES. Fairly uninspired, I should say. The gypsy who sold you one sprig of heather last week for five pounds did rather better.

BELINDA. That was because he belonged to a dying race, and I couldn't bear it. How awful it must be to belong to a dying race. Like the Yaghan Indians. I read somewhere there were only nine Yaghans left, right at the bottom of the world. No, honest! South Chile. Where's the Encyclopedia Britannica? After a while Nature says, "Scrap them," and they just fail, like crops. Isn't it sad? Imagine them. Nine little shrunk people, sitting on green water, waiting to die.

CHARLES (*Grimly*). I am imagining them.

BELINDA. What's the matter with you?

CHARLES. It's a pity I'm not a Yaghan Indian, isn't it? I might get a little attention from you. Yes. Outrageous demand for a husband to make of a wife, isn't it? Attention. Notice.

BELINDA. I notice you, Charles.

CHARLES. Very humorous.

BELINDA. It's not meant to be.

CHARLES. Where were you last night?

BELINDA. Out.

CHARLES. You knew I was bringing someone back.

BELINDA. You said you might.

CHARLES. Well I phoned you from here at six and you weren't home.

BELINDA. Well, so? Did you need me to pour out whiskey or cut his cigar?

CHARLES. That's hardly the point.

BELINDA. It's just the point, I'd say. You always say you want me to entertain your friends, and as soon as you can, you get out the port and send me out of the room. It's incredible, anyway, that a man of your age should be pushing decanters of port clockwise round a dining table. It makes you look a hundred. When I tell my friends, they can't believe it.

CHARLES. I'm sure they can't. But then one would hardly accept their notions of etiquette as final, would one?

BELINDA. Oh, please!

CHARLES. What?

BELINDA. Not your iceberg voice. I can't bear it. "One would hardly say." "I scarcely think." "One might hazard, my dear." All that morning suit language. It's only hiding.

CHARLES. Indeed?

BELINDA. Yes, indeed. Indeed, indeed! People don't say "indeed" any more, Charles. It's got dry rot.

CHARLES. Where were you?

BELINDA. With my friends.

CHARLES. Oh, of course. In some grotesque little coffee bar, I suppose.

BELINDA. Correct, as you would say.

CHARLES. Telling stories about me. The way I talk. The words I use. My behavior at dinner. Very loyal, I must say.

BELINDA. And where were you? In a stuffy old Club, surrounded by a lot of coughing old men with weak bladders and filthy tempers, scared of women and bright red with brandy. How lovely!

CHARLES. That's just disgusting.

BELINDA. You're telling me! . . .

CHARLES. And where are you going now? I mean, where are you *passing* to go to? Another coffee bar?

BELINDA. Perhaps.

CHARLES. Belinda, what does Wife mean?

BELINDA. What?

CHARLES. Perhaps it's a word no one has ever explained to you. Certainly they didn't in that squalid little registry office you insisted on going to, because you couldn't enter a Church. Nevertheless, at the risk of appearing still more pompous, my dear, you made a contract with me. A contract of marriage.

BELINDA. Well, what about it? There's nothing in it that says a woman must drop her friends and take her husband's. I know it's always done, but I don't see it should be. I never promised to cherish those bright red old men in sickness and health. I love my friends: how can I be faithful to you if I'm unfaithful to them?

CHARLES. May I ask what that means?

BELINDA. That you're not my only duty, that's what it means, and I'm not yours. You've got to be faithful to all sorts of people. You can't give everything to just one. Just one can't use everything. And you certainly can't *get* everything from just one. Just because you get sex from a man, it doesn't mean you're going to get jokes as well, or a someone who digs jazz. Oh I know a husband claims the right to be all these things to a woman, but he never is. The strain would be appalling.

CHARLES. Charming.

BELINDA. It's true.

CHARLES. It's not true! You talk about men as if they were hors d'oeuvre: him for the herring, him for the mayonnaise, him for the pickled beetroot.

BELINDA. But that's exactly it! How clever of you to think of a comparison like that. That's marvelous!

CHARLES. Yes, well it's just stupid and immature. I suppose I really shouldn't expect anything else.

BELINDA. Thanks for nothing.

CHARLES. If you were a real woman, you wouldn't find it hard to receive everything from one man. To see everything in him and hope to be everything in return. But it's beyond you, of course.

BELINDA. Thanks for nothing.

CHARLES. Oh stop that!

BELINDA. Then *you* stop it!

CHARLES. Listen to me, and try to understand. Stop fiddling with those flowers.

BELINDA. Well?

(*A slight pause.* CHARLES *collects himself.*)

CHARLES. Let me tell you something. Each man has all of these things inside him: sex, jokes, jazz and many more important things than that. He's got the whole of human history in him, only in capsule. But it takes someone who loves him to make those capsules grow. If they don't grow, he's not loved enough. And that kind of love can only be given by an adult.

BELINDA. Which I'm not. Ta very bloody much! Well, if I'm not, whose damn fault is it? This isn't my home. It's my school.

CHARLES. That's not true.

BELINDA. Oh but yes it is, Charles. Just look at the way you're holding that ruler!

(*A pause. She looks at him seriously.*)

You *were* everything to me once. I thought you were the most fantastic person I'd ever met. I remember the exact moment I fell in love with you. It was half past three on Thursday afternoon February the nineteenth two years ago. You had already explained to me the Theory of Natural Selection, the meaning of Id, Ego and Super-Ego, and were halfway through the structure of Bach's Fugue in C Sharp Minor, Book One, *Well-Tempered Clavier.* I thought to myself, "How can one head hold so much? He's not showing off, these things come up naturally in his conversation." I adored it. The world seemed so wide suddenly. You were the first person who showed me that an intellectual was a marvelous thing to be. Most of my friends are all feelings. They're just like moles bumping about in dark little burrows of feeling. And that was me too. Feeling, feeling all the time—but never getting to understand anything. When you met me, I'd have said or done anything just to join in. I thought people would like me more if I liked what they liked. So I pretended all the

[93]

time. In the end I couldn't tell what I really liked from what I said I liked. (*Frankly.*) You released me from all that. You gave me facts, ideas, reasons for things. You let me out of that hot, black burrow of feeling. I loved you then.

CHARLES (*Dully*). Then.

BELINDA. Yes.

CHARLES. But no longer.

(*A litte pause.*)

BELINDA. I don't know. Living with you has taught me to respect my feelings—not alter them under pressure.

CHARLES. I'm not pressure.

BELINDA. Look, I know I was a pupil before. I admit it—it was good. But you were different then. Now I feel that you hate me half the time.

CHARLES. That's ridiculous.

BELINDA. Well, resent me, anyway. Like an awful headmaster. I feel I have to defend myself in front of you. I feel guilty.

CHARLES. Do you? How extraordinary!

BELINDA. Charles, answer me something.

CHARLES. What?

BELINDA. Do you love me? I don't mean want me, for whatever reason. I mean, love me. Be honest.

CHARLES. Very much.

"Yes?"

BELINDA. Then why the hell don't I feel it? "I'm burning," says the fire. But my cold hands say, "No you're not." Love with me is a great burst of joy that someone exists. Just that. Breathes. And with that joy comes a huge great need to go out and greet them. Yes, that's the word: *greet*. I used to greet you, inside me anyway, forty times a day. Now it's once a fortnight. And always when you're not looking. When you've got your hat on at an angle trying to look jaunty, which you can never manage anyway. It's all so dead with us now.

(*Pause.*)

CHARLES. And he's made you come alive?

BELINDA (*Startled*). What do you mean?

CHARLES. For someone who puts such a premium on her honesty, you make a pretty awful showing. I know, my dear, I know. So there's no need for any of this.

BELINDA. Know?

CHARLES. About him. Your man.

BELINDA. But you can't . . .

CHARLES. But I do.

BELINDA. How?

CHARLES. Never mind how! I may be the pompous headmaster, but I'm not the village idiot. (*Pause.*) Don't you think you'd better tell me?

BELINDA. No.

CHARLES. Is it so painful?

BELINDA. It's not painful at all. But you just wouldn't dig it.

CHARLES. Give me the spade and let me try.

BELINDA. You're marvelous sometimes!

CHARLES. Thank you.

BELINDA. All right. I will. I will. Only you must promise not to interrupt.

CHARLES. Very well.

BELINDA. Just listen and make what sense of it you can.

CHARLES. All right.

BELINDA. I can make none, so we start equal.

CHARLES. Go on.

BELINDA. Well, you know I've been going out by myself for weeks.

CHARLES. I had noticed.

BELINDA. I was trying to think: that's all. Trying to pull myself out of the burrow on my own. I wandered about all over the place, it doesn't matter where. Then one day, about three weeks ago, a man sat down next to me on the bus, turned, and looked me straight in the eye. He was the most extraordinary man.

CHARLES. Handsome. Debonair. The look of a diplomat, no doubt.

BELINDA (Surprised). No, not at all like that. He was a goofy-looking man with spectacles, eating macaroons out of a polythene bag.

(CHARLES *gives her a startled look.*)

He had the funniest expression I ever saw—sort of witty —as if he wanted to wink, but didn't know how. At first I thought he was trying to pick me up, but it wasn't that. It took me a few minutes to work it out. What I was seeing was Approval. Simply that. Do you know, I'd forgotten what it was like to be looked at without criticism? I was so embarrassed I got up and left. He immediately got up too, and followed me. I began to walk very fast down Bond Street, and he walked just as fast behind, until we were both almost running. In the end I dived into the hairdressers and had quite an un-necessary shampoo. When I came out, he was waiting for me, leaning against Cartier's window, sucking an iced lollipop. Since then we've been together every day. I don't expect you to believe what I'm going to tell you, but it's every word true.

CHARLES (*Grimly*). Go on, please.

BELINDA. You're getting upset, aren't you?

CHARLES. Never mind me. Just go on.

BELINDA. I don't want to upset you. I really don't.

CHARLES. On!

BELINDA. All right . . . First let me tell you the oddest thing about this whole affair. I call it an affair because it is one. But do you know, for the whole three weeks since we first saw each other, we haven't exchanged a single word? When I say we meet every day, I don't mean we make a date. All I mean is that like Mary's little lamb, wherever I go he's sure to follow. He's a pure genius at following.

You never see him till he decides to show himself. Then he just pops up—click! Like that!—in a coffee bar or a cinema, or out from behind a statue in the Park. Once I turned round and there he was in the Powder Room at Fortnums. I suppose at the start I ought to have been scared, but I never was. Isn't that odd? All I knew was here was someone who approved of me. Who got pleasure out of just being in my company. Of course I realized he must be the loneliest man in town, but then in a way I was the loneliest girl, so it was sort of fitting. Who was I to complain if he got his kicks following me around? After a bit—and this is the really goofy thing—I began to get mine by following *him*.

CHARLES. What?

BELINDA. The day came when he took over. I'd stopped outside a cinema where there was a horror film, and looked back, as usual, just to make sure he'd seen me go in. And you know, he shook his head. He wasn't going to see that film. He was like you, you see: he didn't really like horror films. Mind you, he'd had a bit of a do with them: I'd made him sit through eleven that week. Instead he turned round, signed for me to follow and marched off to the next cinema. That was the first time I'd ever seen an Ingmar Bergman film. Charles, they're marvelous! This one has a poor old man driving all over Sweden in a motor car, looking for the turning he took wrong, years before. It's pathetic.

CHARLES. No doubt.

BELINDA. It is really. At one point he sees himself in his own coffin!

CHARLES. And this is all you've got to tell me?

BELINDA. Yes. Anyway, as far as what you're thinking's con- cerned. After that the whole thing became marvelous. We never knew what each day would bring. Sometimes I would lead. Sometimes he would. Last week I marched into the National Gallery and stopped in front of Bellini's portrait of a Doge. He was terribly grateful: you know, he'd obviously never seen it. He paid me back by leading me out to Syon House, which is hidden away behind all sorts of slummy things in Isleworth and has a huge hall of green marble, and eight statues life-size in gold! I know everything about him now: the things he likes doing, even what he likes to eat. They're all sweet things—he must be a Greek or something. Actually, he looks a bit Greeky. And he knows everything about me. The other day we were in a shop and he laid that out— (*She picks up the trilby.*) for me to buy. And it's the only hat I don't look stupid in.

CHARLES. Thank you.

BELINDA. Oh, Charles, it's not a question of hats. I've had the most intimate relationship of my life with someone I've never spoken to. What does it mean? . . . When I'm with him I live. (CHARLES *stares at her with a numb ex- pression on his face.*) And because there aren't any words, everything's easy and possible. I share all the time. I share . . . Actually, to be honest, I do feel guilty. I wasn't just passing. I wanted to talk to you. No, not talk. I knew that wouldn't be any good. I wanted to—I don't know—give you something. These flowers. Poor things—they look a bit withered, don't they? I'll get them some water.

(BELINDA *opens the door up right, goes in—screams—runs back into the room. She is followed by* JULIAN *who stands blinking in the doorway.*)

CHARLES. Who on earth are you?

JULIAN (*Surprised*). My name is Cristoforou . . .

CHARLES. I'm afraid the office is closed on Saturday mornings. If you'd care to make an appointment.

JULIAN. We've done that already.

CHARLES. What did I tell you to do?

JULIAN. Go down the fire escape into the Mews.

CHARLES. Well?

JULIAN. I did, but the Mews was so blank and abandoned. There was more life up here.

BELINDA. You know each other?

JULIAN. Your husband, and I are new acquaintances. I don't think it will blossom beyond that.

CHARLES. How long have you been in there?

JULIAN. All the time. It was very illuminating. I mean you being so intimate. If you'd been discussing topics of general interest, I'd probably have gone away.

CHARLES. You mean you listened?

JULIAN. Of course. Eavesdropping is the second thing one is trained in, Mr. Sidley. First shadow your man with your eye, then with your ear. It's an indispensable ability.

BELINDA. Charles, it's him!

JULIAN. He knows it is.

CHARLES. Don't.

JULIAN. I must.

BELINDA. Don't what?

CHARLES. No, please.

JULIAN. It's inevitable.

CHARLES. I forbid you to speak.

JULIAN. You can't. (*To* BELINDA.) I think you should sit down.

BELINDA. Who are you?

CHARLES. I'm your employer. Leave this office at once.

BELINDA. Employer?

CHARLES. Do you hear?

BELINDA. Employer?

CHARLES. Please . . . I ask you as a friend.

JULIAN. You're not a friend.

BELINDA. Who are you? Tell me.

(*A pause.*)

JULIAN (*Matter of factly*). I am a private detective, Mrs. Sidley. Hired by your husband to spy on you.

(*She stares at him in stunned amazement.*)

BELINDA (*Faintly*). No . . .

(*She looks at her husband.*)

CHARLES. It was all I could think of to do. I was at my wits' end.

BELINDA. No. Oh, no!

CHARLES. I know it was awful. But what else could I do? Your behavior was so odd. You must admit that. Any husband would have been suspicious.

BELINDA (*Breaking out*). No! No! No! No! NO!

CHARLES. Belinda!—

BELINDA. Go away! You're filthy! Filthy! . . . I never want to see you again as long as I live!

(*She bursts into tears and collapses on the sofa, sobbing helplessly.* CHARLES *looks on impotently.*)

JULIAN. Well, you heard what she said. Go away.

CHARLES (*Turning on him*). What did you say?

JULIAN. I said go. It's what she wants.

CHARLES. You bloody meddling little wog! I'll teach you to make a fool out of me! Interfere with people's lives! . . .

(*He bounds forward, snatching up a ruler.* JULIAN *snatches up a heavy statuette and threatens him with it. He speaks in a new, authoritative tone.*)

JULIAN. One step more, and I'll interfere with your brains—

(CHARLES *glares indecisively.*)

I mean it, Mr. Sidley. Coshing is the third thing a detective's trained in.

(*Warily, breathing hard,* CHARLES *lowers the ruler.*)

That's better. Now, what have I done to upset you like this?

CHARLES. Only stolen my wife's affections, that's all!

JULIAN. Your wife's affections weren't stolen, Mr. Sidley. They were going begging . . . (*Pause.*) And if you want them back, you must first learn how to get them. For a start, put down that ruler, and go out and walk around the gardens. It's time you waited for ten minutes.

(*When* JULIAN's *back is turned,* CHARLES *makes another attempt to hit him.* JULIAN *whirls round, statue in hand.*)

DO AS I SAY!

(*Even* BELINDA *is startled by this new tone of authority. Speechlessly,* CHARLES *looks from one to the other.*)

BELINDA. Oh Charles, for God's sake, just go!

(*With an attempt at dignity,* CHARLES *tucks the ruler under his arm and marches abruptly into the gardens. There is a pause.*)

JULIAN. So your name is Belinda.

BELINDA. Go away too.

JULIAN. Mine, as you may have heard is Cristoforou. How strange it was to hear your voice for the first time! Even in a scream it sounded charming.

BELINDA. Go with him—go on. You're two of a kind.

JULIAN. You don't know my kind. It's very rare.

BELINDA. It's vile, that's all I know.

JULIAN. Why? What is my crime? The fairy tale Prince has turned back into a frog, is that it? Well, it's no fun for me either. I'd rather keep my magic. Though it's only training in how to shadow, you must admit I do it superbly. I should; I worked at it. Surely you'd like to know why? It's a sad and fascinating story: the making of a detective.

BELINDA. I'm not listening.

JULIAN. Nonsense: you're riveted. Briefly, then, I am a middle-man. Most of my life has been spent making three where two are company. I was hardly out of puberty before I started becoming attracted to other men's wives. Women who were unattainable obsessed me. Usually, out of guilt, I'd work up a friendship with the husband, and take a painful pleasure in being a constant guest in their home. Masochism, you see: very un-Latin. I was always in the middle, getting nothing and being generally in the way. Finally I made myself so unhappy that I had to sit down and think. One day I asked myself this fateful question: "Would you like to know a beautiful, tender, unattached girl to whom you were everything in the world?" And the answer came back: "No!" . . . Revelation! At that moment I realized something shattering about myself. I wasn't made to bear the responsibility of a private life! Obviously Nature never intended me to have one! I had been created to spend all my time in public! . . . This thought simply delighted me. It seemed to account for everything—all the unhappiness I'd ever suffered. Alone, I didn't exist; I came alive only against a background of other people's affairs. (*She turns and looks at him, fascinated.*) Once I realized this, of course, it was the simplest thing in the world to select a permanent career. A detective was the obvious solution. I immediately resigned from Private Life, and became a Public Eye. A dick. Have a macaroon. They ease the heart.

BELINDA. Look: you've got no rights here, so why don't you just dick off to your dick's office?

JULIAN. Oh, how can you talk like that to someone who's been as intimate with you as I have?

BELINDA. Intimate?

JULIAN. Do you deny we have spent three weeks in this city as blissfully as two people ever spent them in its history? Syon House! The Isle of Dogs! Hampstead Heath at six in the morning! Beware! There is no sin more unpardonable than denying you were pleased when pleasure touched you. You can die for that.

BELINDA. What the hell are you talking about?

JULIAN. You and I have exchanged our most personal treasures and that makes rights.

BELINDA. What rights? To make a fool of me?

JULIAN. Is that what I've done?

BELINDA. You know it is.

JULIAN. I don't. I found you aimless in London; I gave you direction. I found you smileless; I gave you joy. Not eternal joy, or even joy for a week. But immediate, particular, bright little minutes of joy—which is all we ever get or should expect. Give up self-pity. It doesn't become you.

BELINDA. Thanks for nothing.

JULIAN. And give up saying that too. It's hideous.

BELINDA. I'll say what I bloody want. It's no business of yours what I say.

JULIAN. Oh, but it is. You are my business. Look into my eye. Come on: look. No, this one.

(*Reluctantly she looks. He stares at her hypnotically, one inch from her face.*)

What do you see? I will tell you. You see one of the Seven Wonders of Nature. The completely Public Eye—which looks entirely outwards. Look into it. Beside this eye, the eagle is blind. The puma needs spectacles. Without immodesty I tell you—this eye possesses the most watchful iris, the most attentive cornea, the most percipient retina in the northern hemisphere. (*He suddenly withdraws it from her scrutiny.*) And for almost a month it has been focused exclusively on you. It has seen more in you than anyone you ever met, or ever will meet. Think of that. And, may I add, it belongs in the head of a man of taste and refinement who has been made to sit through more execrable horror films than anyone should be called on to see in a lifetime of duty. How dared you inflict on me "Werewolves from Mars" *and* "Bloodsuckers from Venus" both on the same day? If that doesn't give me rights, what the hell does?

BELINDA. You're raving mad, aren't you? I should have realized it all along.

JULIAN. Mad! It's not a word I can easily define. And your husband's books aren't much help with it. Look at him . . .

BELINDA. What's he doing?

JULIAN. Beheading the chrysanthemums with his ruler.

BELINDA. That's his way of working off his anger. It's why I have to buy all my flowers off barrows. (*She suddenly bursts into tears.*)

JULIAN. Oh for God's sake don't cry. I can't stand tears. They're so excluding. Please . . . please! Please! Let me dry your eyes. A simple service from a simple friend. Eye-drying while you wait. Voilà! (*He pulls out his handkerchief and showers her with nuts and raisins.* BELINDA's *crying turns to laughter.*) I'm agonized! Utterly agonized! Did I hurt you? I'm sure I did. Nothing can hurt more than a brazil nut aimed with force. (BELINDA *begins to laugh really hard.*) And the carpet! Ohh! Look at them—all over it! I must pick them up before they tread in. (*He falls to his knees on the carpet and starts picking up the raisins and popping them in his mouth as he talks.*) And such a gorgeous rug! Real Bokhara! I can tell. I used to sell them once, door to door, wearing a fez and a stick-on goatee. Some dreadful gimmick of my employers. I looked like an extra out of *Kismet* and sold nothing at all *ever,* not even a welcome mat. (*She stops laughing. He offers her a raisin from the floor.*) Would you like one?

BELINDA. You really are mad. Completely cuckoo!

JULIAN. Cuckoo?

BELINDA. Cuckoo!

JULIAN. Will you give me one more minute before you throw the cuckoo out? Look: this is my last day as a private detective. After your husband gets through with me, I can't hope to go back to Mayhew and Figgis, or anybody else. It's just as well. I was on the point of resigning anyway. You can't imagine how wretched the job is. How unworthy.

BELINDA. I thought you loved it.

JULIAN. I thought I would, too. But I reckoned without my awful desire to be liked. Well, if you're a dick you can't be. If you give your employer bad news he hates you. If you give him good he thinks his money's been wasted. Either way you can't win.

BELINDA. Well, I don't see how I can help.

JULIAN. Oh, but you can. You can get me back my self-respect.

BELINDA. Me?

JULIAN. Yes, Belinda. I've spent three years helping to break up people's marriages. Don't you think it might make it up to them a little if I helped to preserve yours? Let me be honest with you: I'd like to be the first detective to *cement* a marriage.

BELINDA. That's a lovely thought, but I'm not going to stay with Charles just to oblige you.

JULIAN. Why not? You owe me something. You made me betray a job.

BELINDA. I did?

JULIAN. Certainly. I was paid to follow you, not sit down beside you on a bus.

BELINDA. Why did you then?

JULIAN. I couldn't help it. You're a witch. You can throw an acorn at a duck and strike the heart of a man with grief at fifty paces. And unlike all other witches, you can fall in love and still keep your magic.

BELINDA. Fall in love? Who with?

JULIAN. Your husband. You still love him, though I hate to admit it.

BELINDA. You can't know that.

JULIAN. It's obvious from everything I overheard this morning. All you wish is to find your way back to him.

BELINDA. Oh, if there's any finding ways back to be done, it's by him, not me. If you'd known him before, you'd have adored him. He used to be gay—really gay. He'd say hundreds of funny things and then laugh at them himself, which I think is a marvelous sign, to laugh at your own jokes. It means you're in life. Now he's out of it: he's watching all the time; sarcastic, as if something's drying him up.

JULIAN. It is.

BELINDA. What?

JULIAN. Jealousy.

BELINDA. Jealousy? If anyone should be jealous it's me!

JULIAN. What d'you mean by that?

BELINDA. Nothing.

JULIAN. You mean he's unfaithful to you?

BELINDA. Oh no, not really. He takes himself off to a call girl sometimes, somewhere in Notting Hill Gate.

JULIAN. Notting Hill Gate?

BELINDA. Yes, do you know it? It's on the Bayswater Road.

JULIAN. Yes, I know where it is.

BELINDA. Don't be shocked. That's not really unfaithful. He'd die of shame if he thought I knew.

JULIAN. How *do* you know?

BELINDA. A friend of mine saw him going in one day. Her name's Madame Conchita, which is a lovely name for a call girl, isn't it? I mean, you can just see her. Sort of Bayswater Brazilian! He must have found her in the Ladies' Directory.

JULIAN. What on earth's that?

BELINDA. A sort of secret directory of call girls. Privately published. It costs a pound. Charles is riveted by it. He keeps a copy in his desk. I found it there one day.

JULIAN. Oh, you poor thing.

BELINDA. Not at all. It served me right for prying.

JULIAN. And you're not jealous?

BELINDA. Of course not. I think it's very sensible of him. Men should have a change from their wives occasionally. It makes for a happy home. What do you mean he's jealous? What's he jealous of?

JULIAN (*Gravely*). All your personal life which he hasn't given you. Most husbands want to create wives in their own image and resent all changes they haven't caused, all experiences they haven't shared, and—with wives brighter than they are—all new things they can't keep up with. Do you want to know what I think of your Charles?

BELINDA. What?

JULIAN. I think he's pitiful.

BELINDA. He isn't.

JULIAN. He's so afraid of being touched by life, he hardly exists. He's so scared of looking foolish, he puts up words against it for barriers: Good Taste, Morality. What you *should* do. What you *should* feel. He's walled up in Should like in a tomb.

BELINDA. What a marvelous comparison!

JULIAN. It's true, isn't it?

BELINDA. I suppose it is. Poor Charles.

JULIAN. Lucky Charles, to have you. Because he's sick and you're well.

BELINDA. He's not sick. He's just a bit stuffy, that's all.

JULIAN. Sick. If you hear a piece of music, you'll either love it or hate it. He won't know what to feel till he knows who it's by. Sick.

BELINDA. That's true.

JULIAN. Sick.

BELINDA. Go on. More!

JULIAN. You're Spirit, Belinda, and he's Letter. You've got passion where all he's got is pronouncement.

BELINDA. You're not mad. You're not mad at all. You don't miss anything.

JULIAN. Of course. I have a Public Eye.

BELINDA. What else does it see?

JULIAN. That Charles Sidley is half-dead, and only his wife can save him.

BELINDA. How? What can I do?

[111]

JULIAN. You're a witch. You can do anything. Don't you know what you did for me?

BELINDA. What?

JULIAN. You gave me a private life. For three weeks I walked through London, all alone except for you to point the way. And slowly, in the depths of that long silence, I began to hear a wonderful sound: the rustle of my own emotions growing. Incredible sensation: the tickle of original feeling. A detective was dying: a man starting to live. And you showed him that eyes weren't made just for spying through binoculars, and ears weren't created just for listening at keyholes. We are born living, and yet how ready we are to play possum and fake death. You led me out of the dead land, Belinda—where we hide from new experience because we're afraid to alter. Now lead him the same way. Eurydice must lead Orpheus for a change.

BELINDA. Who were they?

JULIAN. Lovers who found their way back from Hades by not looking at each other. Only you do it by not speaking, which is so much better in this babel we're all in. How many more people would stay married if they just shut up and listened and heard each other's heartbeats in the daytime?

(*A pause. They look at one another. He kisses her hand.*)

You gave me the only gift I really needed. Now give it to him.

BELINDA. How?

JULIAN. The same way. In silence.

BELINDA. You mean not speak to him?

JULIAN. Of course. It's his only chance.

BELINDA. But that's impossible!—

JULIAN (*Excited*). Of course! Of course! Of course! (*He goes quickly to the window.*) (*Calling.*) Mr. Sidley! Yes, you! Come up here at once!

BELINDA. What are you going to do?

JULIAN. Do you trust me?

BELINDA. No!

JULIAN. Do you want to return to your marriage?

BELINDA. Yes, I do.

JULIAN. Then do exactly as I say. Do you promise?

BELINDA. I don't know why I should.

JULIAN. Put yourself completely under my orders for a month. I promise in return it'll work.

BELINDA. For a month?

JULIAN. Unavoidable. Promise.

BELINDA. A month's forever.

JULIAN. It's four weeks. Promise.

BELINDA. And I think you really are mad after all.

JULIAN. Promise.

BELINDA. Yes.

JULIAN. You break it and you'll go to hell. Stand there. When he comes in, don't look at him! And whatever happens, don't speak.

BELINDA. Don't speak?

JULIAN. Not a single word.

BELINDA. That's idiotic.

JULIAN. Are you questioning me?

BELINDA. Yes!

JULIAN. Oh well, then, the game's off. There's no fun playing Master and Slave if you're going to question everything.

BELINDA. No, I'm sorry. I'll behave. But not speaking is a bit brutal. You forget I'm a woman.

JULIAN. Well, you'd better get used to it. You're going to have to do it for thirty days. (*She opens her mouth in surprise.*) Ssh. Here he comes. Stand up straight. Look proud! (BELINDA *stands like a statue.* CHARLES *comes storming in.*)

CHARLES. Well, who are *you* shouting at?

JULIAN. You.

CHARLES. Belinda, I think it's time we went home, don't you? We can discuss all this later, at home. Are you coming, dear? (*Pause.*) Belinda, I'm talking to you. (*Pause.*) I'd like you to come home now, do you hear?

JULIAN. It isn't any good, is it, Mr. Sidley?

CHARLES (*Angry*). Belinda!

JULIAN. It's useless to address her. She will not reply. As far as you are concerned, she has renounced speech. I bear her exact and peremptory ultimatum. She is so shattered by your conduct—setting a low, sneaking, prying little wog of a detective to spy on her—that she is leaving you forever.

CHARLES. Belinda! (BELINDA *turns to protest, but is gestured to keep silent by* JULIAN.)

JULIAN. Unless. Yes, you are lucky. There's an Unless. You have one chance of keeping her. But only one. That is—you will take my place in the streets of London. (*Formally.*) You will follow her every day for a month, at a distance of fifty feet, wherever she chooses to go. You will look at whatever she chooses to point at. You will hear whatever she chooses to listen to. You will sit, stand, skip, slide, or shuffle entirely at her will. And for all this month, neither in study nor street, at table nor in bed, will you exchange a single word. (*More easily.*) If there's anything special you want to see and show her, then you may lead. But it had better be good. This is your will, isn't it, Belinda?

(BELINDA *nods.*)

Inexorable, aren't you, Belinda? The alternative is divorce.

(*Nod.*)

Sunderment!

(*Nod.*)

Eternal separation!

CHARLES. Are you done?

JULIAN. Oh yes. End of words, start of action. (*To* BELINDA, *taking her hand.*) Go forth, Eurydice!

CHARLES. Stay here, Belinda!

(*A long pause.* BELINDA *looks between the two men, choosing. Then she smiles at* JULIAN, *picks up her hat and starts to walk out.*)

JULIAN. I suggest the Michaelangelo Coffee Bar for a start. Make him eat a Leaning Tower of Pisa.

CHARLES. Belinda?

JULIAN. No, make him eat two!

(BELINDA *goes.* CHARLES *follows her to the door.*)

CHARLES. This seems a good joke to you, but what are you really doing? You're acting on impulse, that's all. (*He is now out of sight.*) You're living on pure emotion without thought or . . . Belinda . . . Belinda! . . . Belinda? (CHARLES *comes back, slamming door.*) If she thinks I'm going after her, she's mad.

JULIAN. I strongly advise you to follow her, Mr. Sidley.

CHARLES. Do you? Do you indeed? Well fortunately you don't know my wife as well as you think. She'll get tired of this nonsense in an hour. Now get out. And I may as well tell you I'm going to see to it immediately that you are fired.

JULIAN. I'm agonized. Actually I have a much better job to go to.

CHARLES. Indeed?

JULIAN. Yes. Yours. I've come to a decision. While you are outside doing my job, I'll sit here and do yours. Exchange is no robbery, as they say. And even if it is, robbery can be rather stimulating.

CHARLES. Very humorous.

JULIAN. It may well be. I've always had a hankering after the accountant's life. (*Pompous voice.*) "Good morning, Miss Smith: bring me the Sidley Trust file, please." "My dear sir, you have made a great deal of money. You must look to pay a great deal of tax. However, there are one or two—what can one say?—loopholes, I believe, is the vulgar word. I prefer 'modes of avoidance.'"

CHARLES. If you are not out of this office in one minute by my watch, I shall call the police.

JULIAN. If you are not out of this office in thirty seconds by my watch—

CHARLES. Well?

JULIAN. I shall tell your wife about Notting Hill Gate.

CHARLES (*Startled*). What did you say?

JULIAN. I'm not a private detective for nothing, Mr. Sidley. And I did give you warning I was a good one. Once I was sure of your wife's innocence, I took to wondering about yours. So I followed you.

CHARLES. I don't believe it.

JULIAN (*Lightly*). Madame Conchita? Olé! . . . Not exactly my type. We Greeks prefer something more Anglo-Saxon. Let's see . . . There ought to be reference books on the subject. And I'm sure your superb collection must contain at least one encyclopedia on matters sexual. One Almanac of Arcana? At the very least, a Directory.

CHARLES (*His voice faltering*). Directory?

JULIAN. Perhaps it's in the Pornographic Selection.

(*He moves towards the office door.* CHARLES *puts himself between him and it.*)

Ah, closed to the general public.

CHARLES. How dare you?

JULIAN. Go through your desk? Routine procedure. You have fifteen seconds, Mr. Sidley. (*He takes out of his bag a large grapefruit and knife and the cannister of sugar.*) Look: as I told you, I never fail jobs, they always fail me. I can hold the fort here perfectly well for a month. I'll just sit here, turn all comers into Corporations, and let them enjoy themselves. To be an accountant nowadays you simply need a highly developed sense of fantasy. And I'm sure you'll admit I've got that. (*He slices through the grapefruit. The telephone rings.*) Hello? No, this is Mr. Sidley's assistant.

(CHARLES *makes a grab for the telephone, but* JULIAN *dodges.*)

He's on holiday for a month. That's right: one month. (*As* CHARLES *makes another effort to grab it.*) One moment please.

(*He puts down the telephone, and shoves the open receiver in a drawer. He looks very seriously at* CHARLES.)

Look, my dear man, don't be entirely stupid. Your wife's failing love may not be a deductible expense—but it's the only thing you've got. (*A pause.* CHARLES *returns his stare, tacitly admitting the truth of this. He lowers his eyes.*)

(*As if to a child.*)

Go on. Or you'll lose her. (*Indicating the white raincoat.*) And put that on. It may help. Conditioned reflex, you know. If you find any goodies in it, you're very welcome to them.

(*Stunned,* CHARLES *obeys.*)

Reember: one month. I do know your wife, Mr. Sidley, and I know she'll keep at it. But if, by any small chance, she wavers, you must insist. Otherwise—Madame Conchita! Go on, now.

(*He watches, smiling amiably, as* CHARLES *retreats to the door.*)

I'll have the bill sent here, of course. It's more discreet, isn't it?

CHARLES (*Viciously*). One thing, Mr. Cristoforou. If I may remind you, you said that the man my wife met every day was handsome, well-dressed, Mr. Cristoforou. Debonair.

JULIAN. So I did, Mr. Sidley. So I did. I thought it more tactful. I mean any husband can be excused for losing out to a dream figure like that. But to a little reptile like me? . . . (*Taking receiver from the drawer.*) Hello? Sorry to have kept you waiting. Yes, he felt the need for a complete rest. Yes, he had to go—(*Pointedly at* CHARLES. CHARLES *goes.*) Well, permit me to introduce myself. My name is Cristoforou. Julian Cristoforou. Diplomas in Accountancy from the Universities of Cairo, Beirut, Istanbul and Damascus. Author of the well known handbook "Teach Yourself Tax Evasion." What seems to be your particular problem? Income tax? . . . Yes? It's monstrous!

You haven't paid it, I hope? I'm delighted to hear it. Of course not. Paying any tax that is more than one percent of your total income I consider a desperate imprudence. Yes, of course, we have limitless experience in this field. Cristoforou and Sidley. A firm of the very highest. I think you'd better come round and see me immediately.

(*He eats the grapefruit: it is obviously sour. He shakes the cannister of sugar: it is obviously empty.*)

No, my dear sir, I assure you, we won't let the Government touch a penny piece of your money. Not without a battle that will make the Battle of Waterloo look like a Sunday School picnic. Come round in, shall we say one hour. I look forward to it. In the meantime, don't worry about a thing. And if you could bring round with you a pound of granulated sugar, I'd be greatly obliged. Good day to you, sir. Good day.

(*He hangs up as—*

THE CURTAIN FALLS